The Beatings Will Continue Until Morale Improves: Leadership the Antarctic Way

Dr. Roger Podell

DEDICATION

To Sheri

ACKNOWLEDGEMENTS

Several people helped me understand key ideas that were instrumental in writing this book and I owe them many thanks. Accomplished editor and author Janet Podell gave me invaluable suggestions, and Dr. Richard Walter and Dr. Stephanie Tatum of Dowling College were very supportive and helped narrow the focus of my research. Arnis instructor Guro Andrew Filardo taught me to simplify complex concepts into practical strategies that work in application. Kevin Podell shared his insight, which helped me better comprehend the techniques of effective leadership. Kelly Podell introduced me to the all-important concept of FDT. I would also like to thank Dr. Richard Bernardo, Dr. Maria Esposito, Dr. Arthur Friedman, Dr. Diane Impagliazzo, Dr. Albert Inserra, Dr. Robert Manley, Dr. Elsa-Sofia Morote, Dr. S. Marshall Perry, and Dr. Charles Rudiger for their advice and support.

I would also like to acknowledge authors Margot Morrell, Stephanie Capparell, and Dennis N.T. Perkins, who wrote pioneering works that examined Shackleton's leadership. This book attempts to build on their research.

Copyright © 2016 by Dr. Roger Podell
All rights reserved.
ISBN-10: 1494253712
ISBN-13: 978-1494253714
Library of Congress Control Number: [LCCN]
Kambei Publications, Wantagh, NY

CONTENTS

Introduction	1
Chapter 1: Search for the Unknown Land	3
Chapter 2: Fate of the Jeanette	7
Chapter 3: Southern Cross	11
Chapter 4: Discovery	15
Chapter 5: God Has Pity on the Foolish	23
Chapter 6: A Good School	27
Chapter 7: Gjoa Haven	33
Chapter 8: The Last Time I Used Both My Eyes	39
Chapter 9: Forces of Nature	47
Chapter 10: Almost a Miracle	53
Chapter 11: A Variety of Experiences	61
Chapter 12: Somewhat Surprised at Still Being Alive	69
Chapter 13: Doubt Creeps In	77
Chapter 14: I Wish You a Safe Return	83
Chapter 15: Poor Soldier Nearly Done	89

Chapter 16: Penguin Egg Omelets   99

Chapter 17: The First to Be Eaten   105

Chapter 18: All Mothers Will Understand   113

Chapter 19: Do or Die   121

Chapter 20: October Would Be Too Late   129

Chapter 21: Almost Human   139

Chapter 22: A Note for Captain Scott   145

Chapter 23: The Men Who Did Not Fail   149

Chapter 24: Facing South   155

Chapter 25: N25   159

Chapter 26: The Antarctic Model of Leadership   167

Epilogue: What Happened to the Heroes?   179

Bibliography   189

INTRODUCTION

For something so important, leadership gets surprisingly little attention. There is a great deal of discussion about *leaders*: people complain, praise, and argue about them to no end. But leadership, the skill of being an effective leader, is largely ignored, hidden in the shadows of the leaders themselves.

So how do we study leadership with the ultimate goal of improving it? By examining the actions of effective leaders and identifying the techniques they used. Armed with this profound knowledge, we can create a model based on proven, real world success that anyone in a leadership position can use.

To accurately analyze leaders, we must separate them from the numerous outside pressures that impact their decisions. We need a controlled environment where contact with the outside world is virtually nonexistent. Individuals in this situation would have to rely solely on their management acumen—leadership in its purest form. Ideally our setting would be a desolate location, at a time before instant global communication. Luckily for us, there is such a place, and such a time.

From 1897-1922, an era known as the Heroic Age of Antarctic Exploration, an array of sixteen expeditions descended on the frozen Southern Continent, each with a leader responsible for the success of his mission and the lives of his crew. The Heroic Age was a time of bold exploration and scientific discovery. It abounds with stories of heroism, perseverance and selflessness that exemplify the noblest side of the human spirit, while deceit and brutality expose the other side. The numerous diaries, books and photographs from the period tell epic tales of pioneering adventure and exploration. But if we look deeper, there is still more to be discovered. The Heroic Age is a window in time through which we can learn about leadership.

In addition to the copious first person accounts, we have the luxury of hindsight to aid our study. We know the historical context in which the commanders worked, the planning that led to their decisions, and ultimately the consequences of their actions. The appallingly difficult conditions inherent in Antarctic exploration, including an odd combination of life and death crises mixed with months of darkness and boredom pushed the commanders to the limits of their skills, and exposed the essential elements of leadership.

In short, we can improve leadership in the future by learning from successful leaders of the past. All at no cost to you or your organization, because these proven management techniques are *free*. The courageous individuals of the Heroic Age have already paid your way.

Chapter 1

Search for the Unknown Land

Antarctica was originally part of Gondwanaland, an ancient supercontinent that included South America, Africa, and Australia. One hundred and thirty million years ago forces within the Earth's crust forced Gondwanaland to break up, and the tropical landmass that would become Antarctica drifted south, eventually settling at the bottom of the Earth and growing increasingly cold.

Antarctica is like nowhere else on earth. It is by far the coldest place, with temperatures reaching as low as minus 129 degrees Fahrenheit. Larger than both Australia and Europe, Antarctica has over 12,000 miles of coastline, and is surrounded by the treacherous Southern Ocean, which possesses the world's strongest currents. The Transantarctic Mountains separate West Antarctica from the significantly larger East Antarctica, which is home to the Polar Plateau and the South Pole. The Plateau is an immense expanse of ice sitting at an altitude of 13,000 feet, giving Antarctica the highest average elevation of any continent.

Gravity driven katabatic winds constantly cascade down off the Plateau, commonly reaching speeds of 200 miles per hour, and creating uniquely Antarctic blizzards. While the wind moves fast, the ice moves slow, but it too flows down from the Plateau, creating tremendous glaciers that drift between the mountains. The glacial ice ultimately adds to massive ice shelves that glide towards the coastline, ending in giant cliffs that periodically cleave and crash into the sea, forming monumental icebergs.

Over two thousand years ago the ancient Greeks theorized that there was an enormous, ice covered land at the bottom of the Earth. In the sixth century B.C., the mathematician Pythagoras determined the Earth was round. Later, Parmenides, a poet and student of nature, realized that the spherical Earth must receive more direct heat from the Sun's rays at the equator and less at the poles, and hypothesized that the North and South Poles would be frigid.

In 320 B.C., the explorer Pytheas sailed into the Arctic Circle, where he found huge fields of pack ice floating in the ocean and observed the sun shining at midnight. Greek culture and mathematics stressed symmetry, and by 300 B.C. philosophers concluded that the Earth, with so much ice in the north, must have a similar, frozen landmass in the south. They named the northern area *Arktos*, after the bear shaped constellation in the northern sky, and the southern opposite *Ant-Arktos*. The Romans accepted the Greek notion of *Ant-Arktos*, and labeled it *Terra Incognita* or "unknown land" on their maps.

Although the ancients had correctly guessed the existence of Antarctica, it remained undiscovered for centuries. As the Age of Exploration dawned in the late 1400s, European explorers and cartographers believed in the Unknown Land, and assumed it was only a matter of time until it was discovered. In 1520 Ferdinand Magellan's expedition sailed below the southern tips of both Africa and South America, but found no trace of Antarctica. Other expeditions followed, including the Dutch voyage that discovered New Zealand, but the Southern Continent remained elusive.

British explorer James Cook sailed completely around Antarctica without ever actually spotting it. During the summer of 1773 Cook's ships *Resolution* and *Adventure* came within eighty miles of the coastline but encountered pack ice and retreated north. Although the *Resolution* and the *Adventure* were strong vessels, they could not penetrate thick ice.

In 1820, *Terra Incognita* was finally found. On January 16 Russian Captain Thaddeus Bellingshausen spotted one of the colossal ice shelves that cling to the frozen continent. Just two weeks later, British seal hunter William Smith and Captain Edward Bransfield sighted the mountains of the Antarctic Peninsula, which extend out into the ocean near the tip of South America. Smith and Bransfield felt they had been the true discoverers of Antarctica, since they observed actual land, while Bellingshausen had only seen ice attached to land, ice that would eventually fall off into the sea.

Antarctica's coastline was soon surveyed by naval officers, whalers, sealers, and scientists. In January, 1841, explorer James Ross led his ships *Erebus* and *Terror* into a large area of open water now known as the Ross Sea. The sturdy vessels plowed through floating pack ice, and soon Ross could see two mountains, actually twin volcanoes, which he named after his ships. At twelve thousand feet high, Mt. Erebus is the largest of the four major volcanoes on Antarctica, and the only one that remains active. As Ross sailed farther south he reached the incredible ice cliffs that rise two hundred feet straight up from the ocean, and extend as far as can be seen in either direction. Ross called it simply "the Barrier."

Although many sailors had now seen Antarctica, it was not until early 1895, a full seventy-five years after its discovery, that someone actually stepped foot on the continent. Henryk Bull, a Norwegian whaler, sailed the *Antarctic* towards the Ross Sea, and at the head of the sea he came across a rocky strip he called Cape Adare. He was lucky to find it, as ninety-eight percent of Antarctica is covered by ice. A landing party rowed a small boat towards shore. Several men claimed to have been the first person to actually set foot on the continent, including Bull and second mate Carsten Borchgrevink. We will probably never know whose boot first touched the rocks at Cape Adare, but more importantly for future explorers, Bull had located a viable landing point.

Several months later, influential British geographer Sir Clements Markham spoke at the Sixth International Geographical Congress in London, and declared the Antarctic to be "the greatest piece of geographical exploration still to be undertaken." As the new century loomed there was worldwide excitement at the prospect of conquering nature's challenges, and high on the list was the South Pole. A surge of interest in Antarctica began. Scientists felt the continent might provide valuable data in meteorology, biology, and geology. Whalers and sealers sought bases for their hunting operations. Governments were interested in possible military uses and in claiming expansive parts of Antarctica for themselves. Explorers longed to gaze upon never before seen lands, battle the treacherous conditions, and feel the patriotic glory of planting their country's flag at the South Pole. Fame and fortune awaited the first man to reach the very bottom of the earth.

This international fascination with Antarctica lasted for twenty-five years. Sixteen expeditions carried crewmen south from a variety of countries including the United States, Russia, Germany, Sweden, France, Japan, and the two nations that would ultimately participate in a life and death race to the South Pole, Norway and Britain.

Chapter 2

Fate of the *Jeanette*

One of the most important leaders of the Heroic Age never travelled to Antarctica, but his pioneering work in cold weather exploration made him a mentor and inspirational figure to those who did. Norwegian Fridtjof Nansen, brilliant scientist, talented diplomat and Nobel winning humanitarian is perhaps one of the most accomplished individuals of the modern world, and one of the most forgotten.

Nansen's resume includes so many remarkable achievements that it is hard to believe they were all accomplished by a single person. He was actively involved in the establishment of independent Norway, and following the First World War he managed the repatriation of hundreds of thousands of prisoners of war. He helped find homes for millions of war refugees using his invention, the "Nansen Passport," and his diligent efforts helped save millions from starvation in the fledgling Soviet Union. Nansen later orchestrated the largest population exchange in history to alleviate the refugee problem caused by the Greco-Turkish War of 1921-1922. He also worked tirelessly to save what was left of the Armenian population after the genocide of 1915-1923. But before all of that, he was a Polar explorer.

Born in 1861, Nansen was a champion skier and accomplished student in his youth. In 1882, while studying at the Royal Frederick University, he embarked on a five month voyage aboard the *Viking* to study zoology in the Arctic Ocean. When the *Viking* became locked in ice off the coast of Greenland, Nansen first conceived the notion of traversing the Greenland Ice Sheet, which covers much of the interior of the country and is the world's largest ice sheet outside of Antarctica. Six years later, Nansen was completing his doctoral studies in marine biology when he organized an expedition to make the first ever crossing of Greenland.

After sailing to Greenland from Iceland, Nansen and his team of six began the land trek in mid-August. With no other form of transportation available, the team man-hauled, the grueling process of dragging supply laden sledges across the ice. Bitter cold, bad weather and high altitudes slowed their progress, but by late September they had traversed most of Greenland and reached a fjord near the western coast. They used their tent, sledges and local timber to build a crude row boat, and they arrived at the town of Godthaab on October 3.

Nansen received a hero's welcome upon his return to Christiania (now Oslo), Norway in 1889. He later traveled to London, where he received the Royal Geographic Society's Founder's Medal. Armed with his new found fame, Nansen was now in a position to obtain funding for his next expedition—an attempt to be the first man to reach the North Pole.

Nansen had been intrigued by the writings of Henrik Mohn, a Norwegian meteorologist. Mohn had studied the fate of the *Jeanette*, an American vessel that had been crushed by ice while seeking the Northwest Passage. European explorers had been looking for the Passage since 1497, hoping to find a trade route to Asia by sailing from the Atlantic to the Pacific via Arctic waters.

The *Jeanette* had sunk near Siberia in 1881, but objects from the ship had been found on the shore of Greenland, which suggested to Mohn that a formerly unsuspected current existed in the Arctic Ocean. Nansen proposed using this current to reach the North Pole by sailing a ship from Siberia, allowing it to become purposely locked in ice, then drifting toward Greenland. As the ship passed near the North Pole a sledge team with dogs would disembark and make a run north. The

Polar party would be unable to return to the ship, and would have to sledge or row their way back to safety.

A unique ship, the *Fram*, was commissioned for the expedition, and shipbuilder Colin Archer constructed the ship with a rounded hull that would better withstand the crushing power of pack ice. The *Fram* sported other ingenious features, including a retractable rudder and propeller, and a windmill that generated electric power so that precious fuel supplies could be conserved.

Otto Sverdup, a veteran of the Greenland crossing, signed on as Captain, and the *Fram* left Norway in June of 1893. Nansen's plan worked—the *Fram* was quickly caught in Siberian pack ice and drifted slowly towards the North Pole. On March 14, 1895, approximately three hundred and fifty miles from the North Pole, Nansen and fellow Norwegian Hjalmar Johansen left the ship with dog teams. Johansen had been a national gymnastics champion in his youth and was renowned for his power and agility. He was also an accomplished dog sled driver.

Large blocks of uneven ice delayed their advance, and on April 7, after reaching a record north of 86 degrees, Nansen decided their food was running too short to continue. Nansen and Johansen turned south, hoping to reach Franz Joseph Land, an archipelago of small islands in the Arctic Ocean. By the end of May they were only about sixty miles away, but as higher temperatures arrived the ice they were traveling on became unstable. They drifted on ice floes, killing some sled dogs to feed the others. When Nansen and Johansen were forced to leave the ice, they shot the remaining dogs and took to their kayaks. They reached Franz Joseph Land, and survived the winter in a crude stone shelter living on seal, walrus, and bear. Johansen's strength and determination were crucial in helping Nansen withstand the harsh conditions.

In June 1896 Nansen and Johansen, both presumed dead, were accidentally rescued by Frederick Jackson, who was leading the Jackson-Harmsworth Expedition to explore Franz Joseph Land. Nansen and Johansen returned to Norway aboard Jackson's supply ship, and arrived in Vardo on August 7. They were met by Mohn, the meteorologist whose theory of Arctic current Nansen had proven correct. The *Fram* had not been heard from, and Nansen feared the worst, but it arrived in Tromso only days later, and Nansen and Johansen were soon reunited with the ship and her crew. The men of the *Fram* were hailed as national heroes.

Chapter 2 Leadership Concept:

Vision Plus Decision: Nansen spent a lifetime turning his ideas into reality. Not only was he able to conceptualize the crossing of Greenland and the attempt at the North Pole, but he took the key next step of bringing his ideas to fruition. Later, as an international diplomat, he solved immense global problems using the same process.

Chapter 3

Southern Cross

Roald Amundsen was sixteen when Nansen returned to a hero's welcome in Norway following the Greenland crossing. The young man was instantly taken with the excitement and glory of such feats, and he would grow to become the most successful Polar explorer in history. A villain to some, a hero to others, Amundsen's brilliant planning and stoic pragmatism served him well on both ends of the earth.

Born near Christiania in 1872, Amundsen was only fourteen when his father died, and he sought escape from his grief in the adventure stories of the time. He was particularly fascinated by the exploits of Nansen, who later became his mentor, and by the mysterious disappearance of Sir John Franklin in 1845. A British Royal Navy officer, Franklin had already made two trips to the Arctic when he accepted command of an expedition to find the Northwest Passage. Using Ross's sturdy ships *Erebus* and *Terror*, Franklin sailed courageously into the Arctic, never to be heard from again. Ross had fortuitously turned down an offer to command the same voyage.

Still only a teenager, Amundsen decided he wanted to be a polar explorer, following in the footsteps of Franklin and Nansen. He began a regimen of training, including long distance skiing. "At every opportunity of freedom from school, from

November to April, I went out in the open, exploring the hills and mountains which rise in every direction around Oslo, increasing my skill in traversing ice and snow and hardening my muscles for the great adventure," Amundsen later recalled.

Amundsen's mother wanted him close to home and objected to his plans to travel. He acquiesced and enrolled in a local university to study medicine, but following his mother's death in 1893 he left school permanently. That winter he skied over seventy miles alone, and became confident that he was now ready for polar exploration. By 1894 Amundsen had entered Norway's merchant marine and in 1897 he was hired as First Mate of the *Belgica*, the first ship of the Heroic Age to test the Antarctic ice.

The *Belgica* was never supposed to spend the winter anywhere near Antarctica. Belgian Captain Adrein de Gerlache's plan was to sail near the Antarctic Peninsula during the warmer summer months when there was less ice in the water. (In the southern hemisphere, the seasons are opposite those above the equator. Summer is from November to March). The *Belgica* would survey the coastline, then turn north, avoiding the brutal Antarctic winter by spending it in Australia. The following summer the ship would sail south again and continue her explorations.

Captain de Gerlache's plans changed dramatically on March 3, 1898 when early ice trapped the ship. Amundsen and the rest of the crew tried desperately to free the vessel, but the ice would not release its grip. The men of the *Belgica* were about to become the first people to ever spend a winter below the Antarctic Circle.

The multinational crew included men from Belgium, Russia, Poland, Romania and Norway. Amundsen quickly became friends with the ship's surgeon, the American Dr. Frederick Cook. During the thirteen months that the *Belgica* was stuck fast, Amundsen and Cook learned about survival in polar regions, including how to defeat scurvy, a dreaded disease caused by a lack of vitamins and fresh food. When de Gerlache and other officers refused to eat penguin and seal meat because of the taste, they became so incapacitated that Amundsen and Cook were forced to take command of the ship. While doctors at the time were unsure about the cause or treatment of scurvy, Amundsen and Cook discovered that if the men ate fresh meat the illness could be prevented or cured.

Amundsen observed how some of the crew suffered depression and even madness caused by isolation, boredom, and the months of total darkness that occur at the ends of the earth. He quickly realized the importance of keeping the men occupied during these difficult times. Amundsen also found the crew's clothing to be insufficient for the Antarctic winter, and witnessed firsthand the tremendous effort required to man-haul heavy sledges, as Nansen had done while traversing Greenland. To Amundsen, man-hauling was unnecessarily difficult, requiring too much exertion in the bitter cold.

While the crew of the *Belgica* waited for a thaw to release their ship, the *Southern Cross* was sailing south. Financed by wealthy British newspaper publisher Sir George Newnes, the British Antarctic Expedition was commanded by Carsten Borchgrevink, a member of Henryk Bull's pioneering landing party that had first set foot on Antarctica at Cape Adare. Borchgrevink returned to Cape Adare aboard the *Southern Cross* in February 1899. A team disembarked, the first men in history to camp on Antarctica for an entire winter. To avoid being trapped in ice, the *Southern Cross* sailed for New Zealand on the first of March.

The British Antarctic Expedition pioneered the use of prefabricated huts for shelter, and some of the well-designed pine buildings used in the early expeditions still stand today. Borchgrevink, Tasmanian physicist Louis Bernacchi, Norwegian zoologist Nikolai Hanson and seven other crewmen quickly assembled their hut and settled into their new home.

Although the men had scientific work to carry out, as time went on tedium and loneliness took their toll. When the sun disappeared in mid-May, frustrations mounted. Borchgrevink was not well liked, and had trouble maintaining his crew's morale. Conditions improved briefly on July 27 when the sun reappeared, but turned again for the worse when Hanson became ill and died on October 14. Beriberi, a disease caused by absence of Vitamin B1, was the likely cause.

Bernacchi's diary entry expressed the men's "hysterical joy" at the return of the *Southern Cross*. After picking up the men the ship sailed south, stopping at Ross Island, a rocky area accessible via the Ross Sea that serves as an entrance to the Barrier. Borchgrevink and two companions, using dog teams to pull their sledges, traveled inland across the Barrier and reached seventy-eight degrees latitude, a new record for southern travel.

Upon his return to England the Norwegian Borchgrevink proudly proclaimed his accomplishment, but he received an understated welcome from both the press and the geographical establishment. The attention of the nation had already turned to a new, all British expedition to be led by a young naval captain, Robert Falcon Scott.

Chapter 3 Leadership Concepts:

The Power of Preparation: From an early age Amundsen understood the importance of rigorous training. He skied long distances to develop his skills and toughen his body for polar exploration. His dedication to preparation and his aptitude for planning would become keys to a lifetime of successful expeditions.

The Acquisition and Application of Knowledge: Amundsen used his time on the *Belgica* wisely. He received a great education in dealing with the scourges of polar exploration: scurvy, boredom, and man-hauling, and found creative ways to conquer each.

Morale is Not a Given: Borchgrevink and de Gerlache discovered how easily trust, loyalty and optimism can disappear, especially in adverse conditions.

Chapter 4

Discovery

Known as "Con" to his friends and "The Owner" to his crew, Scott was a determined, ambitious, and introspective leader who found himself caught up in an international race for fame in the loneliest place on earth. Scott's remarkable accomplishments assured his legacy as a pioneer, and his tragic demise saddened a nation. Ultimately his reputation as a commander would be attacked, defended, and debated for a more than a century after his death.

Scott was born June 6, 1868, in Devonport, England, near the naval base at Plymouth. His father John was a brewer, and an exception to the Scott family tradition of naval service. Robert's uncle was an Admiral in the British Navy, and the young man seemed destined to a similar career. By thirteen he was in training for a naval cadetship on board the *Britannia*, and by fifteen he had graduated, ranked seventh in a class of twenty-six. By August 1883, Scott was a midshipman aboard the *Boadicea*, named for the warrior queen who led a tribal revolt against Roman occupiers in 60-61 A.D., and later became a martyr and heroine of British nationalism. Almost two millennia later, Scott would be cast in a similar role.

Scott's first step towards the Antarctic occurred in 1887 while training in the West Indies. It was there that Scott was noticed by Clements Markham, retired naval officer, world traveler, and honorary secretary of the Royal Geographical Society (RGS) for the previous twenty-four years. Clements was the guest of his cousin, Commodore Albert Markham, commander of the West Indies Training Squadron. Clements observed a race between three cutters, each with a young midshipman in command. A brief but exciting contest occurred in clear blue waters under sunny skies between Scott, Tommy Smyth, and Hyde Parker. Scott's cutter reached the finish line first, impressing Markham and launching a chain of events that would eventually seal Scott's fate in an ice-covered wasteland at the end of a very different race.

Soon after the cutter contest, Markham spoke to Scott at a dinner party, and was fascinated by his intellect and charm. Although the two did not meet again until a decade later, their relationship had begun, and the seeds of Scott's ability to command had been planted in Markham's mind. Markham's role in Scott's life was dramatic. Like Scott, Markham began his naval training at age thirteen. In 1850 the twenty year old Markham's interest in polar exploration was sparked when he participated in the search for Franklin, whose disappearance in the Arctic so fascinated the teenage Amundsen.

Scott's naval career progressed smoothly, if unexcitedly. He spent four years serving in the Pacific as a sub-lieutenant on the *Amphion*, based on Vancouver Island. In 1891 Scott requested training in a new form of weaponry, the torpedo. Throughout his life Scott often showed interest in new technology, a trait he carried into his years of Antarctic exploration. Mastering a new weapon was also a calculated attempt to further his naval career through specialization.

Scott spent two years at the Naval Torpedo School in Portsmouth, England. Stationed near home, he was able to spend more time with his family, and especially enjoyed being with his mother and younger brother Archie, a soldier in the British Army. Scott also became increasingly aware of his father's financial problems, which would play a crucial role in his future career decisions. In 1894 Scott was assigned to a torpedo ship, the *Vulcan*, stationed in the Mediterranean.

John Scott died in 1897, leaving Robert the primary supporter of the family, with Archie as a secondary source of income. The military did not pay well, however, so Archie transferred to a West African regiment that granted a higher salary, while two of Scott's unmarried sisters moved to London with their mother and opened a dressmaking business. Scott was aboard the *Empress of India* in 1897 when he had a chance meeting with Markham at Gibraltar, off the coast of Spain. Markham later wrote that this meeting confirmed his faith in Scott as a commander.

By 1898 Scott was serving aboard the *Majestic*, the flagship of the Channel Fleet. Archie, home on leave, enjoyed a visit with his brother on board the ship, but within a month Archie died of typhoid he had contracted while serving in West Africa. Scott was deeply affected by his younger brother's death, and left with the sole responsibility of taking care of his mother and unmarried sisters.

Within a year of Archie's passing, Scott emerged from Victoria Station in London and happened to spot Markham walking on Buckingham Palace Road. During the conversation that followed, Scott first heard of Markham's plan for a British expedition to the Antarctic. Burdened with the responsibility of supporting his mother and sisters, depressed over the recent deaths of his father and brother, and ambitious to further his naval career, Scott submitted an application to command the expedition. He had no experience in Polar exploration.

Markham made a few inquiries as to Scott's reputation and accomplishments in the Navy, and received several positive recommendations, but it was likely Markham's instinctual feeling about Scott that moved the young officer to the top of the applicant list. Markham also believed that prior Polar expeditions had mistakenly selected older men as commanders, choosing experience over youth. Ultimately, Markham believed Scott was destined to lead a journey to the Antarctic.

The Royal Society, a different entity than Markham's similarly named Royal Geographical Society, had contributed only one thousand pounds to the expedition, but had managed to secure "co-sponsor" rights with that modest sum. Scott had to be approved by a Joint Committee consisting of members of both societies, including scientists and explorers. The two groups disagreed about the best qualifications for a commander.

Markham and the RGS favored a naval officer, while the Royal Society argued for a scientist.

The ratification process was lengthy and difficult, but Scott was eventually confirmed. This only led to more bureaucracy for Scott to deal with, as the Joint Committee included nine sub-committees, each responsible for a different element of expedition planning. The ship committee agreed to authorize a new vessel, *Discovery*, modeled after the old style whalers but with a larger, reinforced hull. *Discovery* cost more than half of the expedition's budget.

One of Scott's first duties was fundraising. Markham had served as president of the RGS since 1893, but his attempts at private fundraising had been weak. In 1899 Llewellyn Longstaff, retired Army officer, successful businessman, and member of the RGS pledged twenty-five thousand pounds, quickly raising the total collected to almost forty thousand. Though Longstaff was the primary contributor, he did not make a claim for involvement in the design of the expedition. His one request, however, was on behalf of his son Cedric, an army officer who had been impressed by a young merchant mariner named Ernest Shackleton. On Cedric's suggestion, Llewellyn Longstaff met with Shackleton and recommended him to Markham. Naturally, his endorsement carried a great deal of weight.

Shackleton, born in Ireland in 1874, was the oldest boy in a family of ten children that included eight sisters. The Shackleton family had an Irish coat of arms, emblazoned with the motto *Fortitudine Vincimus*, "By Endurance We Conquer." His father, Henry, owned a farm in Kildare, thirty miles from Dublin. When the farm failed, Henry attended Dublin's Trinity College and became a doctor. In 1884, the family moved to London and Henry established a practice.

Ernest was a bright young man, an avid reader who, like Amundsen, had a taste for adventure stories and freedom. He opposed his father's wish that he, too, become a doctor, and instead left home at sixteen to join the merchant marine. "I wanted to be free," Shackleton wrote. "I wanted to escape from a routine which didn't at all agree with my nature and which, therefore, was doing no good to my character." Shackleton spent most of the next eight years at sea, traveling the world, gaining experience, and dreaming of future adventures. The work was difficult and often dangerous. Shackleton witnessed a sailor fall overboard during a storm, and was himself almost killed by a tackle that fell to the deck.

At twenty, Shackleton was serving as the third officer on a passenger ship, and by twenty-four he had qualified for a ship's command. He had also met and fallen in love with Londoner Emily Dorman, and grew eager to improve his financial status so they could marry.

In 1899 Shackleton secured a position with the respected Union Castle Line, which provided him with access to passengers in the upper echelons of society who could help advance his career. He impressed Gerald Lysaght, a wealthy steelmaker, who became a benefactor for Shackleton's later expeditions. In 1900, Shackleton was serving as third mate aboard the *Tintagel Castle*, transporting twelve hundred British Army troops to South Africa to fight in the Boer War. The ship was overcrowded, discipline was strict, and morale was low. Shackleton organized events to raise the spirits of the crew, and volunteered to teach the troops signaling. One crewmember called him the "life and soul" of the ship. It was aboard the *Tintagel Castle* that Shackleton met Cedric Longstaff.

With Llewellyn Longstaff's donation in place for Scott's expedition, and the total nearing forty thousand pounds, the British government offered matching funds of forty- five thousand pounds if another five thousand could be raised. It was, and the British National Antarctic Expedition became a reality.

Scott worked actively to prepare himself for a Polar command. In the fall of 1900, he and Markham traveled by train to Norway to consult with Nansen, whose travels in Greenland and the Arctic made him the world's foremost authority on polar exploration. During the trip, Scott read *Through the First Antarctic Night*, the story of the *Belgica* expedition, written by Amundsen's friend Frederick Cook. Nansen warned Scott about the dangers of man-hauling, and emphasized the importance of using dog teams to pull the sledges instead.

Scott now focused on forming a crew. As a British Naval officer, he naturally sought out mainly naval personnel, even though the expedition was a private venture. The Navy offered the temporary services of lieutenants Charles Royds, Reginald Skelton and Michael Barne, who was selected in part because he was a relative of Markham. Shackleton, a merchant marine, was brought on as a "junior executive."

A key member of the crew was Dr. Edward Wilson, who served the expedition as Junior Surgeon, zoologist, and artist. Born into a Quaker family in 1872, Wilson had been interested in nature from boyhood. He would take long walks observing animals, plants, and rock formations with a keen fascination. In college he studied medicine and eventually became a doctor. A humanistic, moral and religious person, Wilson seemed always to be searching for the best way to help his fellow man. When not enveloped in his studies, he spent time at the zoo, the Natural History Museum, or the National Gallery, indulging his other interests. He also met and fell in love with a young woman, Oriana Souper.

In 1898, Wilson viewed a lecture by Nansen in London, in which the Norwegian explorer discussed his adventures. In 1900, the president of the Zoology Society, Dr. Philip Sclater, suggested Wilson interview for the *Discovery* Expedition. Major General Sir Charles Wilson, Edward's uncle, used his influence with Markham to help his nephew's application move forward. Wilson was appointed, and he married Oriana one month prior to the departure of the *Discovery*.

The crew of the *Discovery* had a combination of Royal Navy men (both officers and seamen), scientists, Royal Marines, merchant marines, and civilians. William Lashly, George Vince, Edgar Evans, and Frank Wild were among the Navy men aboard. Wild claimed to be the great-great grandson of the legendary Captain James Cook, who had circumnavigated Antarctica in the 1770s. Wild's maternal grandfather Robert Cook passed the story down to Frank as part of a proud family history, but it is unknown if Wild was actually related to Cook. True or not, the legend influenced young Frank. By four years old he dreamt of becoming a sailor, and at eight a book on

Arctic adventure caught his imagination, igniting an interest in Polar exploration.

Only a few members of *Discovery's* crew had prior Polar experience. Physicist Louis Bernacchi had done magnetic and meteorological observations on the *Southern Cross* serving under Borchgrevink. Surgeon and botanist Reginald Koettlitz had been in the Arctic, as had second-in-command and navigator Albert Armitage.

Discovery began its voyage on July 31, 1901. The ship stopped at Cowes, on the Isle of Wright, and was toured by King Edward VII and Queen Alexandra. It then travelled south, made several stops, and eventually docked at Lyttleton, New Zealand. Ten days later, *Discovery* suffered its first casualty. As the vessel sailed out of Lyttleton, Seaman Charles Bonner ascended the mainmast to wave to the crowds that had gathered to see the vessel off. Bonner was gripping the weather vane, but when a rod snapped he fell to the deck and perished. Scott suggested that Bonner had been drinking whiskey given to him by Seaman Robert Sinclair. When *Discovery* docked at Port Chalmers for coal, Bonner was buried, and Sinclair deserted.

Chapter 5

God Has Pity on the Foolish

On January 3, 1902, *Discovery* crossed the Antarctic Circle. Soon the ship was in pack ice, forcing its way through with an ironclad hull. Although the ship was in desolate waters rarely travelled by man, bird and animal life were plentiful. Seals lay on the ice floes while gulls, petrels and penguins stayed near the ship. Wilson was able to indulge his interest in ornithology, and created numerous sketches of the birds. Seals were butchered for their meat, and both Scott and Wilson were distressed by the slaughter. "It seemed a terrible desecration to come to this quiet spot only to murder its innocent inhabitants and stain the white snow with blood; but necessities are often hideous and man must live," Scott wrote.

As *Discovery* approached Antarctica, Scott and fifteen crewmembers jammed into a small boat and landed at Cape Crozier, on Ross Island, the rocky area that borders the Ross Sea to the north and the great ice shelf to the south. Scott, Royds and Wilson scaled an extinct volcano to view the vast, mysterious Barrier. The trio soon found themselves in an enormous Adelie penguin rookery, where the adults attacked the men's shins with their beaks and flippers. Wilson was fascinated by the sheer number and behavior of the flightless birds.

From Cape Crozier, *Discovery* then sailed along the coast of Ross Island and made camp in a convenient harbor sheltered by a cape the men named "Hut Point." Stores were unloaded, and a prefabricated hut was built that allowed the crew to live in relative comfort.

The British approached their expeditions with a sense of adventure and a deeply held belief that extreme effort could see them through any difficulty. This outlook led to rather odd decisions and a failure to correctly prioritize. Although the crew desperately required training in both the use of skis and in driving dog teams, time that might have been spent on preparation was often used for experimentation in other, less important areas. *Eva*, a balloon, was set up for a reconnaissance flight. Scott flew first, foolishly tossing all of the sandbags out of the basket when he reached an altitude of 500 feet. Only *Eva's* moorings prevented Scott from literally flying away. "As I swayed about in what appeared a very inadequate basket and gazed down on the rapidly diminishing figures below I felt some doubt as to whether I had been wise in my choice," Scott remembered. Shackleton was next to ride the balloon, but, like Scott, could only see the seemingly endless Barrier. Wilson, far more practical than his counterparts, commented "if some of these experts don't come to grief over it out here, it will only be because God has pity on the foolish."

A February sledging journey from Hut Point to Cape Crozier quickly exposed the weaknesses of the crew of the *Discovery* expedition. Scott had been injured in a skiing accident, leaving Royds and Barne, two of the Naval lieutenants, in command of a team of men and dogs. The sledging proved very slow, and Royds decided he would take two men forward, while sending the rest of the men back to Hut Point under Barne. In order to reach the ship, the men had to cross a range of thousand foot high hills, and just as they achieved the zenith, they were beset by a blizzard. Barne was unprepared for the blinding effects of an Antarctic storm. The party attempted to advance, but retreated to the tents when Seaman George Vince and other men began showing signs of frostbite. Foolishly believing the blizzard would be brief, the men left their sleeping bags outside the tents.

When the wind lessened enough that visibility increased to thirty feet, Barne decided it was time to move again. Being only three miles from the ship, he chose to leave the tents and gear behind and attempt a dash back to the hut. Soon lost and unable to find their way, Barne's men found themselves on a steep, icy ridge that ended in a cliff overlooking the sea. When the storm intensified, the men could barely see each other, and Seaman Clarence Hare was lost from the party. As the team searched for Hare, they stumbled onto a twelve hundred foot slope of ice. Man after man slid down, some catching themselves in small patches of snow.

Vince stopped his descent by grabbing hold of Wild, but when he lost his grip he disappeared over the ridge. Remarkably, Wild managed to catch three other men as they fell towards him. They crawled to the point where Vince had vanished and peered over. Three hundred feet directly beneath them was the sea.

Locating the water gave Wild a better sense of their location. They would be able to return to the ship if they could climb the slope they had just slid down. They began the ascent, desperately clinging to every crevice and foothold. After successfully scaling the slippery hillside, Wild led most of the party back to the *Discovery*, but four men, besides Vince, were still missing.

Wild guided a land search team, while Shackleton commanded a whaleboat that scanned the water for survivors. Three of the missing men were found bewildered and suffering badly from frostbite. Barnes' fingers were permanently damaged. Hare managed to find his way back days later, having gone forty hours without food.

Vince, however, was gone. The events on the ridge and the death of Vince revealed some of the serious problems with the *Discovery* expedition. Besides the obvious inexperience with Antarctic conditions, the sledges were poorly loaded, there were issues with the food, and the clothing was insufficient. Scott later admitted "I am bound to confess…at this time our ignorance was deplorable; we did not know how much or what proportions would be required as regards the food, how to use our cookers, how to put up our tents, or even how to put on our clothes. Not a single item of the outfit had been tested." Many crewmen learned the hard way not to touch metal with bare fingers or eat with frozen utensils.

As winter approached the temperature fell to minus forty degrees, and on April 24 the sun disappeared, leaving Scott and the men of the *Discovery* to reflect on their situation and the tragedy of Vince's death. As the long, dark winter continued, efforts were made to keep up the crew's spirits. Debates were held, theatrical and musical performances were given, and holidays celebrated with special meals. During a full moon there was even enough light for a soccer game. Shackleton edited the ship's newspaper, the *South Polar Times*, while Wilson provided the illustrations. Despite these distractions, the monotony, darkness and cramped quarters took their toll on the men. Soon morale dropped and tempers grew short. "Men don't improve when they live together alone, cut off from all the better half of humanity that encourages decency and kindliness," Wilson wrote. "Some of our mess have quite dropped the mask and are not so attractive in their true colouring."

One event clearly demonstrated the dangers of living in close quarters during months of darkness. Following an argument between two crewmen one went missing, and a search team explored the ice near the ship. The lost man was found hiding, brandishing a crowbar. Knowing a search party would be sent out, he had hoped his adversary would be unlucky enough to find him first.

Chapter 5 Leadership Concept:

The Dangers of Incompetence: Antarctica wasted little time educating Scott and the *Discovery* crew about the hazards of bringing insufficient knowledge, lack of experience, and poor planning to an extremely dangerous environment. An effective leader must be sure that his or her team is prepared to deal with adverse conditions and changing situations.

Chapter 6

A Good School

In June Scott asked Wilson to join him in an attempt to reach the South Pole. Wilson was thrilled, but believed that a third person was essential for the safety of the team. They both agreed on Shackleton. To reach the South Pole, the three man Polar Party would have to travel south on the Great Ice Barrier into areas never before explored.

On August 22, Shackleton and Scott ventured to the summit of nearby Crater Hill, and together they watched the sunrise for the first time in months. Preparations for the Pole trek could now begin in earnest. In early September, Scott began having the men practice sledging with their dog teams. Although they were rapidly gaining knowledge, Scott and his crew were still generally incompetent when it came to surviving in the Antarctic. As reconnaissance and practice teams came back, their reports to Scott were not encouraging. The group led by Royds returned in only two days. Scott wrote that the men were exhausted. "His men have had a great lesson but there is no doubt men cannot face these hard conditions like the officers. Even his party, the best of our people, gave him anxiety at critical times; they don't seem to know how to look after themselves."

The officers, however, performed no better. On September 17, Scott, Barne, and Shackleton left with a dog team and hundreds of pounds of food on a depot laying journey. On their first night out they failed to bury the skirting of their tent in snow, and survived a day long blizzard only by holding the tent in place. Scott recorded "Without exception this was the most miserable day I have ever spent. An inspection...showed that we had all been pretty badly frost-bitten, but the worst was Barne, whose fingers have never recovered from the accident of last year, when he so nearly lost them. To have hung on to the tent through all those hours must have been positive agony, yet he never uttered a word of complaint." During this event most of the dogs withstood the minus fifty degree temperatures by burying themselves in the snow, but Scott let one dog, Brownie, into the tent when he heard the canine whimpering.

On October 30, a support team of twelve men, man-hauling without dogs, left camp to lay depots of food and supplies for the main party. Three days later Scott, Wilson and Shackleton began their journey south with nineteen dogs. Their initial pace was good, the dogs ran well, and they quickly caught up with the support team. On November 10, they covered ten miles and reached the depot at Minna Bluff, a large rocky outcropping on the Barrier. Scott was sufficiently pleased with their progress to send the support team towards the southwest to explore the area known as Victoria Land.

The dogs' performance soon began to lag, however, though Scott was unsure of the cause. The temperature had increased, softening the surface and making sledging more tiresome for them, but it was clear that there was an underlying reason for their decreased energy. As the animals continued to fail, the men resorted to driving them harder. Scott described it as "heart-breaking" work.

As the dogs weakened, they could no longer drag full loads, and Scott was forced to resort to relaying, the agonizing process of moving forward with a half load, going back with an empty sledge to retrieve the other half, and then returning to the last point of forward progress. Using the relay system, three miles were actually traveled for every one that truly advanced them south.

The dogs, in fact, were suffering from food poisoning. Scott had initially planned to feed the dogs biscuits, but Nansen had convinced him to use fish. The fish had been stored on board the *Discovery*, and had turned rotten as the ship passed through tropical climates. "It is easy to be wise after the event," Scott later wrote, "but unfortunately for our dogs, this...escaped our notice, and as there was no outward sign of deterioration it [the fish] was carried on our sledge journey. As a result the dogs sickened...from what one can only suppose was a species of scurvy."

Scott's comment about the dogs demonstrated his agreement with the then commonly held belief that scurvy was caused by food poisoning. In 1905, Scott wrote "I understand that scurvy is now believed to be ptomaine poisoning caused by the virus of the bacterium of decay in meat." An understanding of the actual cause of scurvy, a lack of vitamin C, had not yet been established. Amundsen, however, had noticed a link between the consumption of fresh meat and the avoidance of and recovery from scurvy during the *Belgica* expedition years earlier, something Scott should have been aware of.

On November 27, Scott wrote a passage that revealed the grim realities of their journey:

> Shackleton in front, with harness slung over his shoulder, was bent forward with his whole weight on the trace; in spite of his breathless work, now and again he would raise and half-turn his head in an effort to cheer on the team...Behind him, and obviously deaf to these allurements, shambled the long string of depressed animals...all by their low carried heads and trailing tails showing an utter weariness of life. Behind these, again, came myself with the whip, giving forth one long string of threats and occasionally bringing the lash down with a crack on the snow or across the back of some laggard...On the opposite side of the leading sledge was Wilson, pulling away in grim silence...This then is the manner in which we have proceeded for nine hours today—entreaties in front and threats behind—and so we went on yesterday, as so we shall go on tomorrow. It is sickening work, but it is the only way; we cannot stop,

we cannot go back, we must go on, and there is no alternative but to harden our hearts and drive.

Scott often recorded his feelings about specific dogs in his diary, describing Spud as "daft—there was something wanting in the upper storey," and Jim as a "lazy, greedy villain, up to all the tricks of the trade." Scott admired Kid, who "pulled like a Trojan throughout and his stout little heart bore him up till his legs failed beneath him."

Despite their troubles with the dogs, the trio reached 80 degrees South on November 25, and were very pleased with the achievement. Their enjoyment was short-lived, however, as hunger and the bitter cold began to overtake their thoughts. While all three men were afflicted with snow blindness, Wilson endured the worst of it, but did his best to continue drawing sketches, and would sometimes pull the sledge with both eyes bandaged. As the dogs began to die from starvation and exposure, Wilson fed them to the other dogs, or stored the dog meat for other dogs on the return trip. Scott did not participate when it became necessary to kill the dogs.

By mid-December, Scott, Shackleton and Wilson were consuming far fewer calories than they were using each day. Each of them was suffering from scurvy, with Shackleton showing the worst symptoms. Had they eaten the dogs, they would likely have lessened the effects or avoided the disease altogether, but they chose not to consume canine meat.

After thirty-one days of maddening relaying, Scott made the decision to lay a depot, make a last push for a farthest south record, and then turn north. On December 30, 1902, they reached 82 degrees south, still over 400 miles from the Pole but 250 miles farther than anyone before them had ever achieved. Thus began a life and death race, hopping from depot to depot back to Hut Point. They were ravenously hungry, and the debilitating effects of scurvy were taking their toll. Blizzards lessened visibility and disoriented them. Their sledge meter, a wheel on the back of the sledge, had been damaged, so mileage figures were now estimates at best. On January 10, Scott wrote "We cannot be far from our depot, but then we do not exactly know where we are; there is not many days' food left, and if this thick weather continues we shall possibly not be able to find it." Three days later, almost out of food and desperate, they were thrilled when Scott spied the depot's flag through his telescope.

On January 14, Shackleton began spitting blood, and Scott ordered him to stop pulling. Shackleton was appreciative of Scott and Wilson's sacrifice. "The other poor fellows now have 270 lbs. to pull while I am only allowed to walk along. They are awfully good to me," Shackleton wrote.

On January 15, the men found themselves without their canine companions for the first time in months. As the final dogs had weakened, they had been placed on the sledges and dragged by the men, until finally, when only two were left, the decision was made to sacrifice them. With Shackleton's life in jeopardy, maximum speed was essential. Scott wrote "This was the saddest scene of all; I think we could all have wept. And so this is the last of our dog team, the finale to a tale of tragedy."

On January 18, Wilson's eyes were very bad, and Shackleton had severe chest pains, but a few days later he was able to pull for an hour. By January 25 they could see Mt. Erebus, and by January 28 they were at the relative safety of Bluff Depot. With food for a week they marched on, and by February 3 they were back on board the *Discovery*.

Scott, Wilson, and Shackleton were changed by their shared experience. They had gained a newfound respect for Antarctica and the hardships of long distance sledging. "It was a good school," Amundsen observed, regarding the knowledge the three explorers had acquired during their trek. They had felt the effects of scurvy and the pangs of intense hunger. To Scott, the experience provided an insight into human nature. "Sledging draws men into closer companionship than can any other mode of life. In its light the fraud must be quickly exposed, but in its light the true man stands out in all his natural strength."

Scott sent Shackleton home on the relief ship *Morning*, while he and Wilson stayed in Antarctica for another season of exploration. The three explorers had developed a special attachment to the Southern Continent, despite, or perhaps because of the unique challenges it provides. A deep, permanent bond had formed between Wilson and Scott and while they would return together for another attempt at the Pole, Shackleton would get his chance first.

Chapter 6 Leadership Concepts:

The Power of Perseverance: Considering the failure of the dog teams and the effect scurvy had on the men, it is remarkable that Scott, Wilson and Shackleton made it as far south as they did and made it back alive. While their planning was suspect, their will, both individually and as a team, carried them to unprecedented achievement.

Leading by Example: Scott drove himself at least as hard as he ever asked from any member of his crew, and those serving under him never failed to give their all even in the most dire circumstances. He also showed great empathy for the men and animals who toiled and suffered on his expeditions.

Chapter 7

Gjoa Haven

The year 1904 found Shackleton, Scott and Amundsen in very different situations. Upon his return to England Shackleton married Emily Dorman, and the couple moved to Edinburgh, Scotland. He worked for the Royal Scottish Geographical Society, then dabbled in journalism, politics, and investing. Generally he found the work tedious and unfulfilling, and longed to return to Antarctica and adventure.

Scott had become a national hero but was somewhat uncomfortable with his new found fame. He wrote a book, *The Voyage of the Discovery*, was a much sought after speaker, and addressed thousands at the Royal Albert Hall. Markham was pleased with the results of the expedition, including the farthest south record and the abundance of scientific data the journey had produced. Scott had named a section of Antarctica "King Edward VII Land," and the King met with Scott, naming him a Commander of the Victorian Order.

Amundsen, meanwhile, was on top of the world. After returning from the *Belgica* expedition in 1899, Amundsen had turned his attention to one of the obsessions of his youth, finding the Northwest Passage. Amundsen approached Nansen, who gave his approval and advice. Nansen, as much a scientist as an explorer, conveyed to Amundsen his deeply held belief that research should be an integral part of the expedition. While in the Arctic, Amundsen could determine the current location of the Magnetic North Pole, first discovered by Ross in 1831. Amundsen listened to his mentor and traveled to Hamburg, Germany to learn about magnetism and the use of instruments from Dr. Georg Von Neumayer, a renowned authority on the earth's magnetic fields.

In 1901 Amundsen purchased the *Gjoa*, a strong if somewhat diminutive ship. It took two years for Amundsen, with Nansen's help, to secure financing and fully prepare for the expedition, and on June 16, 1903, the *Gjoa* sailed from Oslo. After stopping in Greenland for fuel, dogs, and supplies, the ship entered the Simpson Strait on September 9, then found a natural harbor on the southeastern side of King William Island in Nunavut, in northern Canada.

Amundsen named the location Gjoa Haven, and spent two years there with his crew of six men. They took careful meteorological and magnetic readings and explored nearby Victoria Island. The small crew included second mate Helmer Hanssen, who would later accompany Amundsen on his quest for the South Pole, and second engineer Gustav Wiik, a young gunner in the Norwegian Navy. Wiik was responsible for taking numerous magnetic readings in a cramped, makeshift observatory built from empty crates. His painstaking observations provided the first proof that the North Magnetic Pole travels in a somewhat regular fashion. Wiik's records would later provide invaluable data to scientists studying solar wind, the stream of charged particles that flow from the sun and cause the magnificent light displays known as aurora borealis near the North Pole, and aurora australis near the South Pole.

Each member of the *Gjoa's* crew was responsible for scientific research, domestic chores and maritime duties. Amundsen believed that an expedition should consist of as few men as possible, thereby keeping each man constantly busy with multiple responsibilities and instilling in each individual a powerful sense of his own importance to the success of the mission.

In November of 1903 the men of Gjoa Haven first made contact with the Netsilik, a local Inuit group, and their friendly relationship soon proved mutually beneficial. The Norwegians learned valuable lessons about survival in polar regions, adding to the knowledge Amundsen had obtained while overwintering in the Antarctic aboard the *Belgica*. The Europeans observed the Netsilik's highly effective use of dog teams and skill at building igloos, but it was their reindeer skin clothing that particularly fascinated Amundsen. He realized that reindeer skin had numerous advantages over woolen European clothes. Even in very cold temperatures the body perspires during exertion, and while wool would become damp, reindeer skin would remain dry. The skins were also wind proof, and gave the wearer an instant feeling of warmth when put on.

From the crew of the *Gjoa* the Netsilik received knives, sewing needles, and other items that had immediate practical use. The nomadic Netsilik actually built permanent structures near Gjoa Haven to stay near Amundsen and his men. Over a century later, in 2012, the claims of brothers Bob Konona and Paul Ikuallaq that Amundsen was their grandfather was disproved by DNA testing. The brothers, both natives of Gjoa Haven, had stated that their father, Luke Ikuallaq, had divulged on his death bed that Amundsen was his father. The DNA test ended two decades of speculation, which had been accepted as fact by some biographers and historians. Some of Amundsen's descendants had even travelled to King William Island to meet the brothers, believing they were related.

As the summer warmth broke up the local pack ice, the *Gjoa* finally departed on August 13, 1905, and only days later arrived at Cambridge Bay on Victoria Island, where eastbound ships were known to have reached. Amundsen had found the Northwest Passage that had eluded European mariners for centuries. As the *Gjoa* continued west, it encountered the *Charles Hanson*, an American whaler out of San Francisco, traveling east. Tears welled in Amundsen's eyes as proof of his discovery emerged through the mist. He met briefly with Captain McKenna of the *Charles Hanson*, who congratulated him on finally solving one of the oldest maritime puzzles.

Amundsen anticipated traveling west along the northern coast of Alaska, then turning south and passing through the Bering Strait. Before the *Gjoa* reached Alaska, however, thick pack ice trapped the ship off Herschel Island, just north of Canada's Yukon Territory, and slightly east of Alaska. Within sight of the *Gjoa* were a number of whalers, also frozen in, and when the ice thickened sufficiently the crews were able to visit each other. Amundsen was anxious to get word of his triumph to the world—he was in debt from the expedition and hoped to sell his tale to the press. When a whaling captain and two Inuit announced plans for an overland journey to a remote Alaskan town known to have a telegraph, Amundsen joined them. The journey took over two months, but on December 5 Amundsen finally arrived in Eagle City, a fur trading post and old gold mining town. Amundsen sent a telegram, which passed through the United States en route to Nansen in Norway. The American press became aware of the story and printed it before Nansen had the opportunity to sell it. Nansen replied to Amundsen with news of his own—Norway had broken away from a ninety year union with Sweden and was now independent. With his discovery of the Northwest Passage, Amundsen was the first hero of independent Norway.

Nansen had been deeply involved in the events that led to Norway's separation from Sweden. He had spoken out on behalf of independence, and when the Norwegian National Assembly decided to search for its own monarch, Nansen was secretly sent to Copenhagen to determine if Danish Prince Carl would consider becoming King of Norway. Nansen persuaded the prince, and after a public vote that chose a monarchy over a republic, Prince Carl and his wife Princess Maud, daughter of British King Edward VII and Queen Alexandra, took the throne. Carl became King Haakon VII.

Amundsen remained in Eagle City for two months then skied back to the still trapped *Gjoa*. He reached the ship on March 13, 1906 to a welcoming crew, but the celebration was short lived. Wiik, the second engineer, became ill with abdominal pain and fever, possibly the result of appendicitis. With no physician on board to treat him, Wiik died on board the ship. He was twenty-seven years old.

In July the *Gjoa* was finally able to emerge from the ice and passed through the Bering Strait in late August. On August 31, the ship arrived in Nome, Alaska, and several days later Amundsen sailed to San Francisco aboard the *Victoria*. He arrived to find a city still reeling from the massive earthquake of

April 18. After Hansen and the rest of the crew arrived with the *Gjoa* there were celebrations, but the ship, too damaged to make the return trip to Norway, was left with the local Norwegian-American community.

Amundsen embarked on a lecture tour in the United States and Europe, using his honorariums to pay off the expedition's debts. Nansen, meanwhile, lobbied the Norwegian government to help Amundsen, and in April, 1907, the Parliament voted to provide financial help that allowed the new hero to finally escape his creditors. With the discovery of the Northwest Passage and his debts finally behind him, Amundsen returned to the United States for yet another lecture tour. This time his fees would be used for a new venture—an attempt to reach the North Pole.

Chapter 7 Leadership Concepts:

Vest Individuals in the Team's Success: Amundsen kept his crews small, and gave each crew member multiple responsibilities. This served two key purposes: it kept them busy during long months of isolation, and it gave each man a powerful feeling of being a valuable, almost indispensable member of the team whose performance was vital to the success of the mission.

Continuously Acquire Knowledge: Amundsen added what he learned from the Netsilik to the information he had obtained while aboard the *Belgica*, quickly making him the most knowledgeable Polar explorer in the world. He was always on the lookout for information that had practical value. In his attempt on the South Pole he would use this expertise to make life easier for his crew, greatly increasing their productivity.

The Dangers of Poor Planning: Wiik's tragic death might have been avoided had a physician been aboard the *Gjoa*, and Amundsen's failure to include a ship's surgeon among the crew is surprising and inexcusable. Although the Antarctic was very treacherous for explorers, many of the deaths during the Heroic

Age were preventable and due to mistakes in judgment or improper planning.

Chapter 8

The Last Time I Used Both My Eyes

While Amundsen's focus was north, Shackleton had his sights set firmly to the south. Inspired by his fascination with Antarctica and his desire to achieve recognition and wealth, Shackleton had spent most of 1907 planning and raising money for an expedition that he would lead to the South Pole. He originally sought to reunite the crew of Scott's *Discovery*, but only two men, Frank Wild and Ernest Joyce, joined him.

From a pool of over four hundred applicants, Shackleton selected the rest of his crew. He knew that the success of a polar expedition relied heavily on the team he assembled, and recognized that the type of men who would be interested in this sort of work were those with what he termed "marked individuality." The realities of a lengthy, isolated voyage meant that these individualists would have to live and work together harmoniously in extremely arduous conditions. Shackleton chose carefully.

Jameson Adams was selected as Second in Command. Though only twenty-seven, Adams had been at sea since leaving home to join the merchant marine at thirteen, and had also served in the Royal Navy. Known for his humor, Adams referred to everyone he met as "mate," and thereby picked up the nickname "Mate" himself. Adams' specialty was meteorology. Eric Marshall served a dual role as ship's surgeon and cartographer.

Welshman Edgeworth David was selected to lead the scientific team. At forty-nine, David was a renowned Oxford trained geologist who had done extensive work in Australia, and taught at the University of Sydney. While researching in the Hunter River area in New South Wales, David had seen indications of ancient glacial activity. He became fascinated by glaciers and Ice Ages, and soon became an authority on both. While on vacation in 1907, David also learned how to ski, a skill that would soon prove very useful.

Douglas Mawson was born in Yorkshire, England, but grew up in Australia, and was destined to become an Australian national hero and iconic figure in Antarctic exploration. A student of Professor David, Mawson was teaching at the University of Adelaide when Shackleton asked him to serve aboard the *Nimrod* as a physicist and surveyor.

Second Officer Aeneas Mackintosh had, like Shackleton and Adams, joined the merchant marine as a teenager. Twenty-eight years old when he joined the expedition, Mackintosh was excited about the prospect of "new lands, novel adventures and original discoveries," he wrote to his sister Bella. "Fancy too if the South Pole is reached—to be one of the party that helped and was attached to it." Mackintosh was eager to be a member of the land party that would overwinter in Antarctica, rather than just a crewman on a ship that would deposit men, and then return to New Zealand for the winter. "Being on the ship is not quite the same thing as we are merely a sort of Ferry boat," he explained.

Shackleton had hoped to purchase the Norwegian ship *Bjorn*, a new, well equipped vessel which had been designed for polar sailing, but lack of funds forced him to purchase the *Nimrod*, an old, small sealing vessel. Captain Rupert England received the *Nimrod* only six weeks before she was due to sail. The ship reeked of blubber and oil, and was missing masts and spars. Preparations were done in a hurried fashion, and by late July 1907 the *Nimrod* was ready. The King, Queen, and other royals toured the ship at Cowes on August 4, and three days later the *Nimrod* departed England for New Zealand.

The ship arrived in Lyttleton, New Zealand in late November and final preparations began. Shackleton had observed the poor performance of dogs on the broken Antarctic surface during the *Discovery* mission with Scott, and planned to use three forms of transportation to cross the ice during the *Nimrod* expedition: dogs, ponies, and a relatively new invention, the motor car. He intended to use the dogs and car to haul supplies over the ice, and rely on the ponies for the crucial trek to the Pole.

Shackleton contacted a dog breeder in New Zealand who had Siberian dogs descended from those used on the *Southern Cross* expedition and purchased nine animals. He also authorized the purchase of fifteen ponies in Northern China and Manchuria, the type that had been used successfully during the Russo-Japanese War (1904-1905) and on the Jackson-Harmsworth expedition (1894-1897, during which Nansen and Johannsen had been rescued by Jackson on Franz Joseph Land in the Arctic). The ponies had been shipped to Australia, and then to New Zealand, where they had been waiting for the arrival of the *Nimrod,* grazing on Quail Island in Port Lyttleton.

Shackleton believed a pony could drag a twelve hundred pound sledge over an uneven trail for between twenty to thirty miles per day. If those figures were accurate, one pony could pull as much as ten dogs, on the same amount of food, and travel farther daily. Captain England admitted the motor car was a novelty, but explained that the machine had special features, including the ability to have the front wheels replaced by runners in soft snow, and gas and oil that had been tested for use in low temperatures.

The animals were loaded onto the *Nimrod* on December 31, and on New Year's Day, 1908, the ship left Lyttleton Harbour. Over thirty thousand people attended the departure. To save fuel, the *Nimrod* was towed south by the steamer *Koonya,* and on January 5 the two ships encountered one of the powerful storms that frequent the Southern Ocean. The *Nimrod* rolled over fifty degrees, severely injuring the pony called Doctor, who was later shot after being unable to stand. On January 6, the wind intensified to hurricane force. Huge waves and heavy seas continued for several days, and the men were forced to live in wet clothes and sleep in damp beds.

On January 11, one of the dogs gave birth to six healthy puppies. The crew of the *Nimrod* used flags to signal the *Koonya* with the good news. When the two ships encountered pack ice soon after, the *Koonya* cut loose the tow cable and returned to Lyttleton.

Twelve days later the *Nimrod* reached the coast of Antarctica, and the Barrier. Shackleton reveled in "the indescribable freshness of the Antarctic that seems to permeate one's being, and which must be responsible for that longing to go again."

Scott had asked Shackleton to use a new, untried route to the Pole, leaving the old *Discovery* route, based from McMurdo Sound, available for Scott's next attempt, planned for 1910. Scott's request could not be taken lightly, as he now had hero status and the support of the Royal Geographic Society. Shackleton, who lacked Scott's reputation as a naval captain or explorer, had to rely on his magnetic personality to garner funds from his backers, and was not in a position to antagonize his financiers, Scott, or the RGS. Shackleton agreed to travel farther east along the Ross Ice Shelf to find a new base.

The *Nimrod* sailed along the Barrier, searching for Barrier Inlet, which would lead them into a natural port, and the opportunity to land far from Scott's McMurdo Sound. They arrived to find that Barrier Inlet was gone, due to miles of the Barrier having fallen into the sea. Shackleton named the new area the "Bay of Whales" because of the large number of leviathans in the vicinity.

Shackleton did not want to go back to McMurdo Sound and even considered wintering on the ice of the Barrier. Wild objected, citing the danger of the ice falling into the sea. When it was determined that the Barrier's edge was, in fact, miles farther south than it had been during the voyage of the *Discovery* (indicating that large sections of ice had broken away), Shackleton accepted Wild's advice and agreed to return to McMurdo Sound, where they could camp on solid rock. Shackleton regretted going against Scott's wishes, but he was unwilling to endanger his crew.

The *Nimrod* was unloaded of stores and supplies as quickly as possible, as Shackleton planned to send the ship back to New Zealand for the winter. While one team built the hut, another sledged fuel, food and equipment across the brittle sea ice from ship to shore. As the brief summer was soon to end, the men worked tirelessly. Twenty-four hour work days were not uncommon.

On the last day of January, while a cask was being lifted out of the hold, a tackle hook slipped, flew across the deck, and struck Macintosh in the eye. "The shock and agony of the wound was pretty bad," Macintosh recalled in his diary. "So this commemorates the last time I used both my eyes." Dr. Marshall operated and removed the eye. Macintosh, who had confided in his sister how he longed to be a member of the land party, would now be sent back to New Zealand for the winter aboard the *Nimrod*. Macintosh was staggeringly disappointed, but Shackleton had little choice.

In addition to Macintosh's injury, there were significant problems with the ponies, which were vital to the success of the mission. After losing Doctor en route, a second pony had become ill and was shot, reducing the total number to eight, and four of those died soon after. While quartered near the hut, the ponies had stood on volcanic sand that tasted of salt due to blizzards covering the ground with sea water. The ponies had eaten the sand, unbeknownst to the crew. When one pony died unexpectedly, an autopsy indicated several pounds of sand in the animal's stomach. Although the ponies' quarters were immediately moved after this revelation, two others died from the same cause, and a fourth died after consuming shavings that had been accidentally contaminated by chemicals. It was noted that the four remaining ponies, Quan, Socks, Grisi and Chinaman had light colored coats, while the animals with darker coats had died.

By early March the crew had made the necessary preparations for winter. Stables had been built for the ponies, and last minute refinements were made to the hut. The plan, as with the *Discovery* expedition, was to begin the march to the Pole in late October, during the warmer summer months, so the men had several months of waiting ahead of them. Shackleton noted that the crew "began to seek some outlet for our energies that would be useful in advancing the cause of science and the work of the expedition." An area of open water prevented a southern depot journey or a trek to the mountains in the west, but an ascent of Mount Erebus, the active volcano approximately thirteen thousand feet high, was deemed possible.

Shackleton believed a successful climb of Erebus would reveal important geological information, and be a source of pride for both the climbers and the rest of the crew. He selected a team of three men, David, Mawson, and Mackay to attempt the summit, with three others, Adams, Marshall and Assistant Geologist Philip Brocklehurst to act as a supporting party. On the morning of March 5 the men began their march, and despite low temperatures and high altitudes, the sextet made good progress. On the night of March 6 they camped at 5,630 feet, as the temperature dipped to minus twenty-eight degrees. The decision was made that the support team would also be able to attempt the summit, except for Brocklehurst, who was suffering from severe frostbite.

While the young scientist stayed behind at camp, the other climbers reached the summit, where they peered into an immense crater, half a mile wide and hundreds of feet deep. As the rising steam instantly froze in the subzero temperatures, incredible shapes emerged, including one photographed in the form of a crouching lion.

The remainder of the winter was spent doing scientific experiments, preparing for the southern journey, and laying depots for the Southern Party that would attempt to reach the Pole. Shackleton selected Adams, Marshall and Wild to accompany him on the trek, and put James Murray, a Scottish biologist, in command of the crew while the Southern Party was away.

Shackleton left orders with Murray that on the following January 15, a party commanded by Joyce would lay a depot near Minna Bluff, then return to the hut. The same team would then go back to the depot with even more supplies, and wait for the returning Southern Party until February 10. If the Southern Party did not reach the Minna Bluff depot by February 10, the depot party was to again return to the hut. If the Southern Party had not returned to the hut by February 25, a search party was to be sent out. Further, lookouts were to be stationed at Observation Hill to keep watch for the returning party, and the hut was to be manned and supplied until March 1.

On March 1 the ship was to sail to the head of McMurdo Sound and observe the ice conditions. If the pack ice was not too thick, the ship could return to the south, but March 10 was set as the latest day the ship could remain in McMurdo Sound, for fear of it being trapped in the ice.

Towards the end of October, final preparations were made. The sledges and other equipment were checked to make sure they were in proper working condition. The remaining ponies appeared healthy and ready for the journey. The men of the Southern Party wrote letters to their families, to be delivered in case they did not return.

Chapter 8 Leadership Concepts:

Choose Your Team Carefully: Shackleton selected the crew of the *Nimrod* from over four hundred applicants, looking for highly motivated, talented individualists who could also be team players. He showed that through a shrewd and thorough selection process, you can find skilled, unique individuals who can function as a cohesive unit.

Look for Opportunities to Raise Morale: Shackleton was keenly aware of the importance of keeping up morale, and of ways to elevate it. The successful ascent of Mt. Erebus by David's team was a perfect example—it lifted the spirits of the entire crew.

Chapter 9

Forces of Nature

On October 28, 1908, Shackleton's Southern Party, along with a support team, began their quest to reach the South Pole. The weather was good during the early phases of the trip, although the perilous task of navigating around the deep crevasses that permeate Antarctica slowed the team considerably. Bouts of snow blindness began to plague the men, which further delayed their progress. The condition causes extreme pain, followed by double vision, then blurred vision, until finally the eyes become so swollen they close. Although the members of the Southern Party carried goggles, they often chose not to use them, as the lenses would fog up due to the perspiration formed by the exertion of pulling the sledges. Fogged goggles made it impossible to see the highly dangerous crevasses that lurked beneath their feet.

On the evening of November 9 the men of the Southern Party heard a loud, deep sound that caused both the air and the ice to shake for about five seconds. Shackleton and his crew believed the cause of the vibration was the breaking off of an enormous mass of ice from the Barrier into the ocean. Although the men did not need a reminder of the power of nature, they were startled to hear and feel the calving of the ice, which they knew must have occurred at least fifty miles away.

On November 21 the Southern Party traveled over fifteen miles, and Shackleton was pleased with their progress. One of the four ponies faltered to the point of being unusable, however, and was killed. Some of the meat was taken on the sledge, while the rest was stored for the return journey.

On November 26, Wild wrote in his diary that he believed the team would reach the Pole, but was unsure they would survive the return journey. The next day, Shackleton, Marshall, Adams and Wild passed the point at which Scott, Wilson and Shackleton had been forced to turn back in 1902 during the *Discovery* Expedition. Shackleton wrote "It falls to the lot of few men to view land not previously seen by human eyes." Two days later, the pony Grisi fell several times during the march. Suffering from snow blindness and not eating, he was shot, his meat stored in a depot. On December 1, another animal weakened to the point of being unable to pull a sledge and was killed, leaving the team with only one pony, Socks.

On December 4, the team of four men and one pony passed between two towering granite pillars that marked the entrance to the huge glacier that would gradually lead them up to the Polar Plateau. Wild estimated the glacier to be thirty miles wide and one hundred miles long.

On December 7, as Shackleton, Adams, and Marshall dragged one sledge, Socks dragged the second sledge behind him with Wild aboard. The Shackleton team walked unaware over a snow covered crevasse, but as Wild followed, the "weight of the pony broke through the snow crust and in a second all was over." A call for help from Wild brought his three companions running. They discovered the sledge hanging over the edge of a crevasse, with Wild desperately holding on. Wild was immediately pulled to safety, but Socks was gone. Shackleton wrote, "We lay down on our stomachs and looked over into the gulf, but no sound or sign came to us. A black bottomless pit it seemed to be."

Wild had survived because the swingletree, the cross bar connected to both the pony and the sledge, had snapped and dropped into the abyss with Socks, allowing both Wild and the sledge to separate from the falling animal. Marshall noted that he had previously suggested replacing Socks' swingletree with one that was stronger, reinforced and copper bound. Had this suggestion been acted on, the swingletree would likely not have broken when Socks fell into the crevasse, and Wild and the sledge would have been lost.

The death of Socks was costly to the chances of the team reaching the Pole. Although the pony was exhausted and probably would have been shot that night, his loss cost the team hundreds of pounds of vital meat. On the positive side, the sledge and the vital gear it carried, including two sleeping bags, had survived.

Without pony power, the men were now pulling five hundred pounds per two man sledge. They were burning five thousand calories per day, while consuming only three thousand, trapped in the vicious logic of Antarctic mathematics. Man-hauling required the men to drag their food with them (except for food that was stored in depots). The energy needed to carry the weight of the food plus the equipment and fuel needed to cook it caused the men to exert more calories than the food itself could provide. To add more food simply increased the weight, which in turn meant more exertion. Thus man-hauling meant starvation diets, even when consuming thousands of calories per day.

For the next few weeks, the four men of the Southern Party ascended the glacier Shackleton had dubbed the "Highway to the South." They anxiously avoided hidden crevasses, tripped over uneven ice, suffered numerous cuts and bruises to their hands, knees, and shins, dealt with painful snow blindness and frostbite, and steadily climbed over 9,800 feet while dragging hundreds of pounds of food and equipment behind them. On Christmas Day, 1908, they celebrated with a special dinner.

Once the Southern Party had ascended the glacier that led to the Polar Plateau, they hoped to find an even surface and a clear path to the Pole. The expanse, however, was not as smooth as Shackleton had imagined. "If a great plain, rising every seven miles in a steep ridge, can be called a plateau, then we are on it at last," Shackleton wrote. Once they passed 10,200 feet, the Plateau finally began to flatten out, and Shackleton anticipated covering fifteen miles per day in their final push to the Pole. A shortage of food and debilitating altitude sickness prevented them from achieving this optimistic goal. On December 29, when they were only one hundred ninety-eight miles from the Pole, Shackleton wrote, "My head is very bad. The sensation is as though the nerves were being twisted up with a corkscrew and then pulled out." The body temperature of the men had fallen to ninety-four degrees.

Rations had been cut dramatically. As food became scarce, Shackleton took steps to guarantee equal distribution at meals. Each man, including Shackleton, served as cook for a week on a rotating schedule. During meals, the cook would pour hoosh (boiling hot stew) into each man's pannikin (a small metal cup), and stack biscuits in four piles. If someone suggested that one pannikin had less than the others, the hoosh was reapportioned. When all four agreed the servings were equal, one man would turn around so he could not see the food. Another man would point to a pannikin and a group of biscuits and say, "Whose?" The man who could not see the food would say the name of one of the other three, and this process continued until all the men had their food, and each man believed that if there was a smallest portion, it had been given randomly.

On New Year's Day, 1909, the team traveled over eleven miles, but it was a difficult hike, uphill and in soft snow. On January 2, the quartet climbed to over 11,000 feet above sea level. At one hundred sixty-two miles from the Pole, Shackleton began to think about turning back. "We are not traveling fast enough to make our food spin out and get back to our depot in time…I must look at the matter sensibly and consider the lives of those who are with me. I feel that if we go on too far it will be impossible to get back."

By January 4, Shackleton knew that the end of their journey was near, as his team was weakening fast. The men were now dragging only seventy pounds each over a relatively flat surface, but they found the work much harder than three weeks earlier when they were dragging two hundred and fifty pounds up the glacier. That night the temperature dropped to minus twenty-four degrees. On January 6, Shackleton declared they would make one final push the next day, plant the flag as far south as possible, and then begin the return journey north. In his diary, Shackleton wrote "I would fail to explain my feelings if I tried to write them down, now that the end has come. There is only one thing that lightens the disappointment, and that is the feeling that we have done all we could. It is the forces of nature that have prevented us from going right though. I cannot write more."

There was no push south on January 7 or January 8, as a blizzard forced the four men to stay in the cramped confines of their tents. On January 9, the blizzard finally subsided, and the final trek was made. They reached a point ninety-seven miles from the Pole, and planted the Union Jack. "Then I took up the flag, and although it was perhaps the worst moment that I have ever experienced, gave the order to turn back," Shackleton recalled. Later, he asked his wife, Emily, "A live donkey is better than a dead lion, isn't it?"

Chapter 9 Leadership Concepts:

The Importance of Fairness: With food scarce, Shackleton put procedures in place to ensure that every man in the Southern Party felt he was being given equal rations. This evenhandedness prevented the bitterness and anger that even a hint of inequality would have caused. Even under mundane conditions, employees desire fairness and expect equal treatment from management.

The Good of the Men: Shackleton was desperate to reach the South Pole, but was not willing to sacrifice the lives of his men to achieve his goal. Leaders can ask a lot from their people, but ultimately must put those people first, ahead of their own ambitions.

Chapter 10

Almost a Miracle

The next few weeks were a struggle of enormous proportions as the party undertook what Shackleton called "a series of races against death." With no food left, the men would march to a depot, where there would be just enough food to keep them alive long enough to reach the next cache. The depots themselves were difficult to locate in the vast, often featureless white expanse.

The quartet made good time, racing over the ice with a gale at their backs, and nearly destroying the sledge in the process. Shackleton was immensely proud of his companions, who never complained despite their cold and hunger. He recalled later that his personal suffering was magnified by his feelings for the men. "It is impossible to convey to anybody the mental and physical strain that I, as leader, went through then. Although they were so splendid I felt that every hardship they suffered was a reproach to myself."

On January 21, Shackleton took ill with an irregular pulse and fever. By January 24 the team was down to two days' food supply, with the next depot over forty miles away. Two days later, with their food completely gone, Marshall gave each man a forced march tablet consisting mainly of cocaine. By the morning of January 27, the depot was only a few miles away, but Adams, Shackleton and Wild were completely exhausted.

Marshall went on alone, surviving three separate falls into crevasses by lunging for the edges of the ice. By the time Marshall brought food back to his companions, they had gone forty hours without eating. Although they were grateful for the food, the pony meat they ate gave Wild dysentery, which made him weaker still.

On January 30, Wild wrote in his diary that Shackleton "privately forced upon me his one breakfast biscuit, and would have given me another tonight had I allowed him. I do not suppose that anyone else in the world can thoroughly realize how much generosity and sympathy was shown by this; I do. By God I shall never forget it." Later in the journey, while Shackleton and Wild lay in their tent, bitterly cold and starving, Shackleton asked Wild if he would return with him to the Antarctic. Wild wrote "without any hesitation I replied 'yes!' We then went on to discuss details. Shackleton was sure that he could raise sufficient funds in Australia to return [this] year."

On February 2 the men were pleased to reach another depot, and were now only three hundred miles from the hut and safety. As they lived on starvation rations, their thoughts and dreams turned to food. Shackleton's February 17 diary entry reads in part "We all have tragic dreams of getting food to eat, but rarely have the satisfaction of dreaming that we are actually eating."

By February 21 they were still forty-five miles from Bluff Depot, and their lives rested on Joyce's successful laying of food there. "Each time we took in another hole in our belts we have said that it will be all right when we get to Bluff Depot," Shackleton wrote. Although they could see Mt. Erebus, they were not exactly sure where the depot was, and there were no tracks to guide them. With no food left, their spirits began to sink.

Mirages are common in Antarctica, as light is bent and reflected by endless stretches of uneven ice covered surfaces. Just when all hope seemed lost, a mirage brought the depot flag into view just over the horizon. Wild spotted it, and Marshall took a quick bearing. As suddenly as it appeared, it was gone. Shackleton recalled the event as "the most mysterious thing that has ever happened to me."

On the morning of February 22, the men found recent, northbound tracks of men, sledges, and dogs. Wild wrote in his diary, "Good old Joyce." On February 23, twenty-five days after reaching the farthest South ever recorded, the weary men of the Southern Party finally reached Bluff Depot, and food.

Rejuvenated, they pressed on towards the hut and their shipmates. On February 27, they covered twenty-four miles and were getting close to the hut, but Marshall's dysentery worsened, and he was unable to continue. Shackleton decided to make camp, leave Marshall with Adams, and try to reach the hut with Wild. They took only two sleeping bags, a compass, and food rations for one day. They began marching at 4:30 in the afternoon. At 11:00 the next morning, they were still going. Neither Shackleton nor Wild had slept, and they were now completely out of food. At 2:30 on the afternoon of the 28th, they encountered open water, and were forced to take a longer, more difficult approach to the hut. The welcomed sight of men in the distance made their sledge feel lighter for a few moments, but they soon realized that what they thought was a relief party was merely a group of penguins.

Shackleton and Wild abandoned the sledge and sleeping bags and made a dash for the hut. At 7:45 p.m. they finally reached they their destination only to find it deserted. A letter written by Edgeworth David stated that the men had been picked up by the ship, which would wait off Glacier Tongue until February 26, then turn north. Shackleton and Wild looked at each other in silence. It was February 28.

The letter also stated that all the men were safe. Shackleton was relieved, but also confused. If all were indeed safe, why had his orders not been followed? The hut was supposed to be manned until March 1.

Shackleton and Wild scavenged the hut. "It was with very keen anxiety in our minds that we proceeded to search for food. If the ship was gone, our plight, and that of the two men left out on the Barrier, was a very serious one." Hoping the *Nimrod* was still nearby, they attempted to set fire to a small hut, but it would not light. Next Shackleton and Wild attempted to tie a flag to the hilltop cross that honored Vince, who had plunged to his death off an icy slope during the *Discovery* expedition. Their fingers were simply too cold to tie the knots, and they retreated to the hut. Shackleton and Wild found some food and oil, and built an improvised stove. They spent a bitterly cold, sleepless night in the hut without their sleeping bags, wrapped in roofing material.

Captain Evans, formerly in command of the tow ship *Koonya*, and now of the *Nimrod*, had ignored Shackleton's orders. Evans was concerned that the *Nimrod* might become trapped in ice, and had kept her sheltered off Glacier Tongue since February 25. He believed Shackleton and the rest of the Southern Party were dead, as it had now been one hundred and twenty days since they left, carrying food for only ninety-one days. On March 1, with the water relatively clear of pack ice, Evans sailed the *Nimrod* to Hut Point to land a party to search for bodies, but instead found Shackleton and Wild waving a flag.

By 11:00 a.m. Shackleton and Wild were aboard the *Nimrod*. They ate lunch with the men who hours earlier had been preparing to look for their remains. By 2:30 that afternoon Shackleton was back on the Barrier, leading the relief party to rescue Marshall and Adams. Shackleton had not slept for fifty-four hours, but he insisted that as commander of the expedition, it was his duty to direct the rescue team. Marshall and Adams were found alive. Shackleton's Southern Party was soon together again on board the ship, having survived the furthest journey south to date.

Shackleton learned that Joyce and his team had stocked Bluff Depot on January 26, and then returned on February 8 to surprise the Southern Party with some apples, mutton and other luxuries. Joyce's orders were to leave the depot on the 10th if Shackleton and his men did not appear. Joyce discussed the situation with his team and decided instead to lay a series of flags to direct the Southern Party towards the depot. They then traveled due south, hoping to rescue the men, but all they found were some southbound hoof prints and sledge tracks, made by the Southern Party months earlier. Joyce and his men followed the tracks of their shipmates for seven hours until they disappeared. The next day they turned around and headed north.

They doubted they would ever see the members of the Southern Party alive, as they were eighteen days late.

Shackleton realized that the system of using ponies and man-hauling had failed. "Our experience made it obvious that a party which hopes to reach the Pole must take more food per man than we did, but how the additional weight is to be provided for is a matter for individual consideration," he wrote. Joyce's team, meanwhile, had been very successful using dog teams, and on the return journey from Bluff Depot the dogs pulled extremely well and traversed thirty-three miles. In a remarkable feat of luck, Joyce's dog team, with Marston running alongside, passed over a crevasse just as it opened. A photograph of the scene shows sledge tracks on either edge of the crevasse. Joyce confided in Shackleton that their escape was "almost a miracle."

While the Southern Party had been away, David, Mawson, and Mackay became the first people to reach the Magnetic South Pole. Shackleton took great pride in their accomplishment, and was especially impressed by David, who at age fifty had led the expedition. Without the benefit of ponies or dogs, the team had made a sledging journey of over twelve hundred miles.

On March 4, The *Nimrod* pushed through the forming pack ice of McMurdo Sound and narrowly escaped being trapped in the Antarctic winter. Shackleton wrote, "We watched the little hut fade away in the distance with feelings almost of sadness, and there were few men aboard who did not cherish a hope that someday they would once more live strenuous days under the shadow of mighty Erebus."

On March 22, 1909, the ship anchored in a bay on Stewart Island, New Zealand. "No person who has not spent a period of his life in those 'stark and sullen solitudes that sentinel the Pole' will understand fully what trees and flowers, sun-flecked turf and running streams mean to the soul of a man," Shackleton wrote. "We landed on the stretch of beach that separated the sea from the luxuriant growth of the forest, and scampered about like children in the sheer joy of being alive...It seemed as though nothing but happiness could ever enter life again."

On June 14 Shackleton arrived at Charing Cross Station in London to cheering crowds. He attended lavish parties, made public speaking appearances describing his adventures, received widespread admiration, and was knighted by King Edward VII. He traveled to Christiania, Norway, where he spoke to university students who honored him with a torchlight parade. Amundsen stood next to Shackleton on a hotel balcony as he addressed the crowd. Shackleton was well aware of the Norwegians' interest in polar exploration, and their skill with skiing and dog sleds.

Amundsen was terribly impressed with Shackleton's accomplishment. "Seldom has a man enjoyed a greater triumph; seldom has a man deserved it better," Amundsen wrote. "Shackleton's exploit is the most brilliant incident in the history of Antarctic exploration." Amundsen noted that the men of the *Nimrod* had, "more than any of their predecessors…succeeded in raising the veil that lay over Antarctica. But a little corner remained."

How different the lives of Shackleton, Amundsen, Scott and so many others might have been had Shackleton managed to conquer the remaining ninety-seven miles and reach the Pole. Amundsen and Scott would have had little reason to continue their quest for a prize that had already been won. Ironically, though Shackleton failed to reach the Pole, he came so close as to prove that it could be done, and ignited a spark in his two rivals that would determine their fates.

Chapter 10 Leadership Concepts:

Take Pride in Your People, and Responsibility for their Success and Well Being: Shackleton was immensely proud of his men. He knew firsthand the hardships they were silently enduring and blamed himself for their suffering. Shackleton felt a tremendous responsibility to keep his men alive and worked tirelessly to preserve their safety.

Selflessness Builds Trust and Loyalty: Shackleton's act of giving his food to Frank Wild, and the loyalty Wild felt in return, exemplifies how leaders can build loyalty and trust through selflessness. In spite of the bitter cold and terrible hunger he had endured, Wild unhesitatingly agreed to return to the Antarctic with Shackleton.

Chapter 11

A Variety of Experiences

Scott had returned from the *Discovery* expedition in 1904, and by 1906 he was considering another attempt at the South Pole. In December of that year, he met Kathleen Bruce, a free-spirited, artistic young woman who contrasted and complemented Scott's serious personality. The couple married and was expecting their first child when word arrived in March 1909 that Shackleton had almost reached the Pole, but had been forced to turn back. Scott saw his opening.

Amundsen, meanwhile, had been planning an expedition to the North Pole. In 1907 he had written to Nansen asking to use the *Fram* for his proposed expedition. Nansen was torn—he was considering his own attempt at the South Pole aboard the *Fram*, and at forty-six he might soon be too old to attempt such a long, strenuous journey. Nansen, however, was not actively preparing for an expedition, and his time was consumed by his role as Norway's ambassador to England, where he lived apart from his wife Eva and their five children. He was willing to leave the diplomatic position, but only to spend more time with his family, not to embark on a dangerous journey that would take years to complete. Later that year Nansen tendered his resignation, planning to be home by Christmas. Tragically, Eva, his wife of eighteen years, took ill with pneumonia and died on December 9, before Nansen returned.

Nansen agreed to let Amundsen use the *Fram*. Amundsen's notoriety, coupled with the support of his famous mentor, allowed him to secure financing, including a sizeable sum from King Haakon and Queen Maud. Amundsen spent 1908 and most of 1909 planning his expedition, selecting his crew, and refitting the *Fram*. Then, everything changed. On August 31, 1909, the *New York Herald* ran a front page headline stating that Dr. Frederick Cook, Amundsen's shipmate on the *Belgica*, had reached the North Pole in April 1908. Trapped in the Arctic, Cook had been unable to get word of his accomplishment out to the world any earlier. One week later, on September 7, the front page headline of *The New York Times* exclaimed that explorer Robert Peary had discovered the North Pole in April 1909, a year after Cook. Peary, however, argued that Cook had not actually achieved the Pole, and a so began a heated debate about one of the coldest places in the world.

Although Amundsen publicly supported his old friend Cook in the dispute, in the end the result would not matter. Regardless of which explorer could prove, or at least sway public opinion to believe that he had been first, Amundsen's chance at the North Pole was gone. But Shackleton had shown the South Pole was attainable, and Amundsen already had funding, a ship, experience, and desire.

On September 13, 1909, less than two weeks after the *Herald's* headline ran, Robert Falcon Scott publicly revealed his intentions to attempt another journey to the South Pole. The next day Kathleen gave birth to their first child, Peter Markham Scott.

As soon as he learned about Scott's announcement, Amundsen decided to change course. Although the northern trip had been publicized as a scientific expedition of the North Polar basin, and Amundsen's backers had funded him on that basis, he saw nothing wrong with altering his destination. "It was therefore with a clear conscience that I decided to postpone my original plan [to go north] for a year or two," Amundsen later recalled. "I know that I have been reproached for not having at once made the extended plan public, so that not only my supporters, but the explorers who were preparing to visit the same regions might have knowledge of it. I was well aware that these reproaches would come." He believed his financiers would support his decision after the fact.

"Nor did I feel any great scruples with regard to the other Antarctic expeditions that were being planned at the time. I knew I should be able to inform Captain Scott of the extension of my plans before he left civilization, and therefore a few months sooner or later could be of no great importance," Amundsen wrote. He also chose not to inform Lieutenant Nobu Shirase, leader of the Japanese expedition aboard the *Kainan Maru*, though he knew the Japanese team posed little threat in a race to the South Pole.

Amundsen initially kept his decision a secret from everyone except his brother Leon, whom he trusted implicitly. Amundsen later felt it necessary to confide in Thorvald Nilsen, who would serve as commander of the *Fram*. "The way in which he received it made me feel safe in my choice of him," Amundsen recalled. "I saw that in him I had found not only a capable and trustworthy man, but a good comrade as well." One name noticeably omitted from Amundsen's list of confidants was Fridtjof Nansen.

Scott, meanwhile, began to build his team. *Discovery* veteran Dr. Edward Wilson joined the expedition largely out of personal allegiance to Scott, but also because of his distaste of civilization. "I am getting more and more soft and dependent upon comforts, and this I hate," he wrote. "I want to endure hardness and instead of that I enjoy hotel dinners." Wilson would serve as head of the scientific staff and expedition artist. Teddy Evans, a lieutenant in the Royal Navy, was named second-in-command. Evans had been the Second Officer on the *Morning*, the relief ship that brought Shackleton back to England after his illness during the *Discovery* expedition.

Captain Lawrence Oates, also known as "Titus" and "Soldier," was an army officer from a wealthy family. An experienced horseman, Oates was assigned to care for the Manchurian ponies Scott planned to use in Antarctica. "Soldier" Oates had distinguished himself during the Boer War when a platoon under his command was attacked. Despite being outnumbered, Oates' men held their position for over eight hours until reinforcements arrived. Oates suffered a severe bullet wound during the skirmish which left him with one leg shorter than the other.

Lieutenant "Birdie" Bowers was a veteran of the Royal India Marine and had served in Burma. Bowers reveled in hard work and British nationalism. He was interested in Antarctic exploration and had read Scott's book about the *Discovery* expedition. During a chance meeting with Clements Markham, Bowers talked his way into an appointment to the 1909 expedition without a formal interview. Scott also selected *Discovery* veterans Edgar Evans, William Lashly, and Tom Crean, all strong sledgers. *Discovery* crewman Frank Wild, recently returned from Shackleton's *Nimrod* expedition, declined Scott's invitation.

Scott charged Wilson with choosing the large scientific contingent of the crew. Wilson picked a varied group that included a surgeon from the Royal Navy, Edward Atkinson, meteorologist George Simpson, and geologist and *Nimrod* veteran Raymond Priestley. Australians Frank Debenham and Griffith Taylor were also hired as geologists, and Canadian Charles Wright, a Cambridge physicist, rounded out the scientific team. Bernard Day, another *Nimrod* crewman, was hired to care for the motorized sledges, which, it was hoped, would make travelling over the ice significantly easier. Scott, though not a scientist, had a keen interest and supported Wilson and his team as much as possible. He arranged for the *Terra Nova* to be equipped with the latest scientific instruments.

One of the most interesting members of the crew was Apsley Cherry-Garrard, who, like Oates, was from an affluent family. Cherry-Garrard's father had served with distinction in the Indian Mutiny and the Zulu Wars, rose to the rank of Major General, and was fifty-three when he married Evelyn Sharpin, a doctor's daughter. Apsley, their only son, enjoyed life with his sisters on the large family estate when he was home from prep school.

1907 was a pivotal year for the twenty-one year old Cherry-Garrard, who was studying classics and rowing crew at Oxford. His father died after having suffered from a lengthy and debilitating illness. Cherry-Garrard's relationship with his father had been one of love and admiration. As a child, he had been impressed with tales of his father's bravery, and as a young man Apsley longed to live up to the legend his father left behind.

In September, Cherry-Garrard first met Wilson and Scott at the home of his cousin, publisher Reginald Smith. Cherry-Garrard took an immediate interest in Scott and Wilson's plans to go back to the Southern Continent, and Wilson was impressed by Cherry-Garrard's intelligence. After learning that Scott was indeed returning to Antarctica, Cherry-Garrard wrote to Wilson in October 1909 expressing his interest in participating in the expedition, but was rejected. The following year, Cherry-Garrard offered one thousand pounds to become a member of the crew. This was a significant amount, twice that given by the Royal Geographical Society, and equal to the donations of wealthy benefactor Llewellyn Longstaff and the New Zealand government. Again the young man's application was rejected, but he impressed Scott by stating that the expedition could keep the money regardless. Eventually Scott selected Cherry-Garrard to join his team.

Herbert Ponting, a well-traveled photographer who had covered the Spanish-American and Russo-Japanese wars was hired as expedition photographer. Ponting had read Scott's book about the *Discovery* expedition while aboard the Trans-Siberian railway in 1907, and met with Scott in London in 1909.

It was Ponting who first mentioned Cecil Meares, son of a British Army officer, to Scott as a potential crew member. Meares had spent time in northern India, the Himalayas, claimed to have experience driving dogs in Siberia, and had likely served as a British spy. Scott ordered Meares to travel to Siberia, obtain animals, and transport them to New Zealand. Meares purchased thirty-one dogs, nineteen ponies, and hired two young Russians, Demetri Gerof and Anton Omelchenko, who had experience with dogs.

Meares would be in charge of the dogs in Antarctica, while Oates, with his cavalry background, would be responsible for the ponies. Oates was not available to help Meares select the ponies, as he was still serving with his cavalry regiment in India. Oddly, Meares based his selection process partly on Scott's suggestion to favor light colored animals. Scott was aware that light colored ponies on Shackleton's *Nimrod* expedition had fared better than ponies with darker coats, even though their deaths were related to eating sand and tainted shavings, and had nothing to do with their coloring.

Scott worked long hours to secure funding and a ship. He had hoped to use the *Discovery* again, but was unable to, and eventually purchased a slower ship, the *Terra Nova*, for his journey. He traveled with Kathleen to Norway to meet with Nansen, and discussed his plan to attack the Pole with a combination of Manchurian ponies, dog teams, motorized sledges, and man-hauling. As always, Nansen believed skiing and dog teams were the best forms of Polar travel. He introduced Scott to Norwegian Tryggve Gran, an expert skier who Scott quickly realized would make a valuable addition to the *Terra Nova* crew. While in Norway Scott tried to contact Amundsen, but not surprisingly was unable to set up a meeting.

Unlike Scott, Amundsen built a crew specifically designed for the task of reaching the Pole. "I intended to try to get people with me who were specially fitted for outdoor work in the cold. Even more necessary was it to find men who were experienced dog drivers; I saw what a decisive bearing this would have on the result," Amundsen explained.

Amundsen sought men with a "variety of experiences" and skill sets that were ideal for a team trying to win a polar race. Helmer Hanssen and Sverre Hassel were expert dog team drivers and first rate navigators, while Olav Bjaaland was a dexterous carpenter and world class skier. Oscar Wisting was a veteran sailor who had served on whalers in the Arctic. These four highly talented men ultimately made up Amundsen's Polar Party.

Nansen asked Amundsen to consider selecting Fredrik Johansen. Johansen had proven himself an accomplished explorer as Nansen's partner during their attempt on the North Pole in 1895 aboard the *Fram*. Although Johansen brought valuable experience, he had also battled alcoholism for years. Amundsen reluctantly agreed, and Johansen was reunited with the *Fram*.

On June 1, 1910, the *Terra Nova* left London, and arrived in Melbourne, Australia on October 12. It was here that

Scott received a brief but powerful telegram from his Norwegian competitor: "Am going South. Amundsen."

"Scott's plan and equipment were so widely different from my own that I regarded the telegram...rather as a mark of courtesy than as a communication which might cause him to alter his program in the slightest degree," Amundsen wrote. "The British expedition was designed entirely for scientific research. The Pole was only a side-issue, whereas in my extended plan it was the main object. On this little detour science would have to look after itself."

Chapter 11 Leadership Concepts:

To Win, Build a Team that is Task Specific: Amundsen assembled a crew specifically designed to win the race to the South Pole. The men were first rate dog team drivers, skiers, carpenters and navigators—the exact skills required for success. Scott's varied crew was more well rounded, but less suited for a high speed competition.

Provide the Tools Necessary to do the Job: The *Terra Nova* expedition was as much dedicated to scientific discovery as it was to reaching the South Pole. Scott made sure Wilson and his scientific staff were outfitted with the most modern equipment.

Does the End Justify the Means? Was Amundsen's delay in exposing his plan ethical? It could be argued that he was merely seeking a tactical advantage, but did he have a moral duty, in the interest of fairness, to announce his intentions to Scott earlier? Leaders must decide if the Machiavellian approach is right for them.

Chapter 12

Somewhat Surprised at Still Being Alive

Scott was angry about Amundsen's message, but decided to keep to his original plan and timetable. Equipped as he was, there was very little he could have done to alter his strategy even if he wanted to. The *Terra Nova* made a final stop in New Zealand before heading south in late November. By December 31, 1910, the crew had sighted the Southern Continent.

Scott brought his ship into the natural harbor of McMurdo Sound. As the ship was unloaded, the varied dangers of Antarctica became immediately apparent. Ponting, the photographer, ventured onto an ice floe to capture images of killer whales. His subjects quickly turned on him, and Ponting made a desperate dash across floating pieces of ice to escape the orcas. "The ship was within sixty yards, and I heard wild shouts of 'Look out!' 'Run!' 'Jump, man, jump!'" Ponting later recalled. "But I could not run; it was all I could do to keep my feet as I leapt from piece to piece of the rocking ice, with the whales a few yards behind me...I wondered whether I should be able to reach safety before whales reached me; and I recollect distinctly thinking, if they did get me, how very unpleasant the first bite would feel, but that it would not matter much about the second."

Further trouble ensued when one of the three motorized sledges fell through a thin patch of ice. Scott was distressed that such an expensive vehicle had been lost so quickly, but there was nothing he could do. A prefabricated hut, fifty feet long, twenty-five feet high and insulated, was erected. The structure was large enough to provide a comfortable home for the crew for an extended stay. Once the hut was in place, preparations began for the journey to the Pole. Dog teams were taken out for practice and exercise. Often sledges would be driven across bridges of packed snow that covered perilous crevasses. If the bridge was strong enough to support the weight of the men, dogs, and sledges, the team would traverse the chasm, never knowing how close they had come to disaster.

On one occasion, the snow bridge did not hold. A team driven by Meares and carrying Scott fell, and the dogs plunged into the crevasse. The sledge stopped on the edge, allowing Meares and Scott to quickly jump clear. Eleven dogs, tangled in their harnesses, were hanging down, suspended between the sledge on one side of the gap, and the leading dog, Osman, on the other. "Why the sledge and ourselves didn't follow the dogs," Scott wrote, "we shall never know." Cherry-Garrard and Wilson ran to assist. Osman crouched down, using all of his power to keep from being dragged into oblivion. Had he fallen, the sledge and all the dogs would likely have been lost.

Two dogs fell out of their harnesses and landed on a ledge some sixty-five feet down, where they actually went to sleep. The tangled dogs fought one another, using the backs of other dogs to stand on. "Choking sounds from Osman made it clear that the pressure on him must soon be relieved," Scott wrote. Using some rope and tent poles, Scott and Meares were able to secure the harness and free Osman, then haul the other dogs to the surface.

Two dogs remained on the ledge below. Scott prepared to be lowered by rope to rescue them. Wilson objected, believing the attempt to be too dangerous. If someone had to go, Wilson argued, then he should be the one. Scott, however, would neither abandon the dogs nor allow anyone to go in his place. Scott was lowered into the abyss, and the dogs, who were very happy to see him, were saved.

On January 14, the *Fram* reached the Barrier, and soon entered the Bay of Whales, the same area that Shackleton had decided was too dangerous to winter on during the *Nimrod* expedition. Shackleton had feared it that if the area was just ice, rather than ice sitting atop land, it could calve from the shelf at any moment and leave the men stranded on an iceberg, or thrown into the frigid water. Amundsen disagreed. "With one exception," Amundsen wrote, "we were all at this time of the opinion that the part of the Barrier...rested on land, so that any fear of a sea voyage was quite superfluous." (The location was, in fact, located on a section of ice that broke away from the shelf in May, 2000).

Although the Barrier is impenetrable for most of its enormous length, Amundsen was able to find remarkably easy access at the Bay of Whales. A convenient spot was located for unloading, where a small hill of snow led from the sea ice to the top of the Barrier, which was only twenty feet high at this point. Stores were quickly removed from the ship, as were the one hundred and sixteen dogs. By January 17, work on the hut had begun, and the dog teams pulled sledges carrying materials from the ship to the building site. "It is no exaggeration to say that everything went like a well-oiled machine," Amundsen wrote proudly. "The dogs worked splendidly, and their drivers no less, and as fast as the materials arrived our future home rose into the air." Amundsen named his camp Framheim.

Scott, meanwhile, was finalizing plans for various journeys that would leave from his base at Cape Evans. A geological team would study glaciers, while a team led by Naval Commander Victor Campbell would be brought by the *Terra Nova* east along the Barrier, past the Bay of Whales, to King Edward VII Land, where they would explore unknown areas. The ship would then head north and return to New Zealand, to avoid being trapped in winter ice.

Teams were also dispatched to lay depots of food for the trip to and from the Pole. Oates and Scott led a team of thirteen men, eight ponies, and twenty-six dogs to create depots, but the ponies responded poorly to the harsh conditions, and several died on the trek. Oates urged Scott to push the animals as far south as possible, but Scott disagreed. "I have had enough of this cruelty to animals, and I'm not going to defy my feelings for the sake of a few days march," Scott told Oates. The army officer replied, "I'm afraid you'll regret it, sir." They laid a large cache nicknamed "One Ton Depot" one hundred and thirty miles from their base at Camp Evans, but thirty miles farther north than originally planned. Although Scott dismissed it at the time, the added distance would be of grave importance later on.

The *Terra Nova* sailed east, without Scott, en route to King Edward VII Land. Unable to find a landing place, they were returning towards McMurdo Sound when they entered the Bay of Whales to harbor for the night of February 3 and encountered the *Fram*. "Our watchman had just gone below for a cup of coffee," Amundsen wrote," and when he came up again, there was another ship lying off the foot of the Barrier. He rubbed his eyes, pinched his leg, and tried other means of convincing himself that he was asleep." In what must have been a surreal meeting between the competing crews, Amundsen and two of his men ate lunch aboard the *Terra Nova*, while Campbell and two Englishmen visited the *Fram*. The men of the *Terra Nova* observed the vast number of dogs and a demonstration of the discipline and precision of the Norwegian dog teams.

On February 10 Amundsen began his first depot laying journey. As this was the first attempt ever made to go inland from the Bay of Whales, it was also a reconnoitering mission. "This first inland trip on the Barrier was undeniably exciting," Amundsen wrote. "The ground was absolutely unknown...what kind of country should we have to deal with? Would it continue in this boundless plain without hindrance...or would Nature present insurmountable difficulties?" Surprisingly, Amundsen doubted, albeit briefly, if dogs were the best option for Antarctic travel. "Were we right in supposing that dogs were the best means of transport in these regions, or should we have done better to take reindeer, ponies, motor-cars, aeroplanes, or anything else?" Any doubts he had about the dogs were soon answered, however. "We went forward at a rattling pace; the going was perfect."

Scott returned from the Barrier on February 22, and learned of the presence of the *Fram*. "One thing only fixes itself definitely in my mind," Scott wrote. "The proper, as well as the wiser, course for us is to proceed exactly as though this had not happened."

Scott was growing quickly dissatisfied with the enigmatic Meares. "Bit by bit I am losing all faith in the dogs and much in Meares...[he] hates exercise and doesn't inspire confidence to see the thing through." Scott further noted that Meares "rather imagined himself racing to the Pole and back on a dog sledge...It is evident that I have placed too much reliance on his experience."

The *Terra Nova* expedition was multifaceted, including scientific research, exploration of other sections of Antarctica, and the bid for the Pole. While preparations for the trek to the Pole continued, the Northern Party, led by Lt. Campbell and including the geologist Raymond Priestly, was brought to Cape Adare in East Antarctica to geologize and survey the area. They lived in Borchgrevink's hut left over from the *Southern Cross* expedition, near a rookery of millions of Adelie penguins.

Amundsen's team continued depot laying journeys well into March, as the temperatures began to noticeably decline. He was determined to lay depots at least as far south as 82 degrees, and he did, arriving there on March 8. In order to reach that goal, however, the dogs had been pushed to their limits. "It was the utmost my five dogs could manage," Amundsen wrote. "Indeed...it was already too much. They were completely worn out, poor beasts. This is the only dark memory of my stay in the South—the over-taxing of these fine animals—I had asked more of them than they were capable of doing."

With the depots laid, the crews settled in to wait out the cruel Antarctic winter. Amundsen was actually excited about the impending months of piercing cold and constant darkness. "What my comrades thought about the winter that was approaching I cannot say; for my part, I looked forward to it with pleasure," he wrote. "When I stood out there on the snow hill, and saw the light shining out of the kitchen window, there came over me an indescribable feeling of comfort and well-being. And the blacker and more stormy the winter night might be, the greater would be this feeling of well-being inside our snug little house."

Amundsen, who had witnessed depression and madness among some of the crew of the icebound *Belgica*, knew he had to keep his men engaged to maintain their mental health. "It was not my intention that we should spend the winter in idleness—far from it. To be contented and well, a man must always be occupied...My special aim was that everyone should be happy and comfortable, so that, when the spring came, we might all be fresh and well and eager to take up the final task."

Each man had specific duties. Army Lieutenant Kristian Prestrud and Johansen took astronomical readings, while Hassel was in charge of the fuel supply of coal and wood. Bjaaland and master carpenter Jorgen Stubberud were given the task of reducing the weight of the sledges. By shaving down the wood that made up each sledge, the weight was greatly lowered, while aluminum was added to support the joints.

At the *Terra Nova* base at Cape Evans, Wilson, with his strong interest in ornithology, approached Scott with a request to explore the penguin breeding ground at the remote Cape Crozier they had discovered during the *Discovery* expedition. Wilson wanted to observe penguin behavior, as it was believed that male penguins cared for the eggs, but this had not been proven. It was also unknown when exactly penguin eggs hatched. Wilson was further interested in conducting embryonic studies on the eggs to test the suspected connection between reptiles and birds. Scott allowed Wilson to make the journey, assigning Cherry-Garrard and Bowers, two strong man-haulers, to accompany him.

The three men left camp on June 27. The trek, made largely in darkness and in temperatures that plummeted to minus 77 degrees, was so difficult that Cherry-Garrard aptly titled his book about the experience *The Worst Journey in the World*. It took the trio nineteen days to arrive at their destination. They collected five eggs, but only three survived the trip back to the hut at Cape Evans. Wilson, Cherry-Garrard and Bowers returned to their camp frostbitten, undernourished, exhausted, and "somewhat surprised at still being alive."

On August 24, the sun, which had disappeared for four months, reappeared. The focus of both teams now turned to the journey to the Pole. "The day for our actual start could not be fixed; we should have to wait until the temperature moderated somewhat," Amundsen wrote. He relayed a typical conversation among his men from that time: "I'd give something to know how far Scott is today." "Oh, he's not out yet...It's much too cold for his ponies." "But how do you know they have it as cold as this? I expect it's far warmer where they are among the mountains, and you can take your oath they're not lying idle. Those boys have shown what they can do."

Chapter 12 Leadership Concepts:

Quality Preparation Leads to Increased Productivity: Amundsen kept his men busy, happy, and as comfortable as possible while they waited out the winter. Each crewman was given specific, important duties to focus on. He wanted them mentally and physically ready for the push to the Pole. Scott, conversely, allowed Wilson and Bowers, key members of his team, to undertake an exhausting, dangerous, and unnecessary mission during the dead of winter, weakening them for the upcoming race.

Selflessness Inspires Trust and Loyalty: Scott's act of saving the two dogs from the crevasse, and his refusal to let anyone else attempt such a dangerous task, demonstrated his selflessness, kindness, and bravery. Scott would not ask anyone to take a risk in his place. These qualities inspired the same type of trust and loyalty in Wilson that Frank Wild felt for Shackleton.

Chapter 13

Doubt Creeps In

Amundsen and his men were anxious to get started for the Pole, but they had to wait for warmer weather. As September of 1911 arrived, temperatures ranged from -43 degrees to -63, but when -20 was recorded on September 6, it "felt quite like a mild spring breeze," Amundsen noted. The increase in temperature presented an opportunity. "Every man ready; tomorrow we are off," he wrote.

"Every man" was not quite accurate. The experienced Johansen voiced his concern that it was too soon in the season to begin the journey, and that colder temperatures might return while the men were exposed on the Barrier. Amundsen disagreed, an on September 8 a party of eight, including Johansen, left Framheim for the Pole. Despite early success with the dog teams, temperatures soon descended back into the minus sixties, and both men and dogs suffered greatly. By September 14 the decision had been made to turn around. The following day it was discovered that both Hanssen and Stubberud were having significant problems with their feet. Specifically, their heels had frozen.

The return journey was intensely difficult. Several dogs who could not keep up with the pace of the teams were let loose and left to die on the ice. Instead of travelling as a group, the teams went at their own pace. At four in the afternoon the first two sledges, led by Hanssen and Wisting reached Framheim, followed by two more at six, then two more at six-thirty. "The last did not come in till 12:30 a.m.," Amundsen wrote. "Heaven knows what they had been doing on the way!"

In fact, the last two teams belonged to Johansen and Prestrud, who had two frozen heels and was not doing well. Johansen had rescued the young lieutenant and returned him safely to Framheim. The next day, Johansen voiced his opinion of Amundsen, the foolishness of an early season trip, and the fact that the other teams had raced ahead and left Prestrud behind. Amundsen's response to Johansen's comments was to remove him, Prestrud and Stubberud from the Polar Party. "Circumstances had arisen which made me consider it necessary to divide the party into two," Amundsen wrote, without directly addressing the issue of Johansen. The three were given a new assignment, exploration of King Edward VII Land, and Prestrud would be in command. "Henceforward, therefore, we worked, so to speak, in two parties. The Polar party was to leave as soon as spring came in earnest. I left it to Prestrud himself to fix the departure of the party he was to lead; there was no such hurry for them—they could take things more easily."

On October 19, the amended Polar Party left Framheim. Hanssen, Hassel, Bjaaland and Wisting each drove sledges led by thirteen dogs each. Amundsen sat on Wisting's sledge. "Anyone who had seen us would no doubt have thought a Polar journey looked very inviting," Amundsen wrote. The dog teams were remarkably efficient, and in four days they covered ninety-nine miles.

Amundsen had developed a plan that would bend Antarctic mathematics to work in his favor. His strategy was to kill the weakest dogs en route on a predetermined schedule, then feed them to both the men and the remaining dogs. In this way, Amundsen combined his means of transportation and his food supply into one source, and eliminated the need to carry extra food which would add weight to the load.

Scott had devised his own strategy for reaching the Pole. His team would traverse the Great Ice Barrier, with its dangerous crevasses, climb the 9,000 foot Beardmore Glacier that flowed down through the Transantarctic Mountains, and finally cross the windswept Polar Plateau to the Pole, the same route Shackleton had used during the *Nimrod* expedition. Scott spent many hours contemplating the details, including how the combination of ponies, dogs, motorized sledges and man-hauling could be best used to cross the varied surfaces of Antarctica.

Scott planned to take a Southern Party of twelve men, with ponies, towards the Pole. Support teams using motorized sledges would go ahead of the main group, leaving depots of food and cooking fuel for them. Other support teams using dogs would travel with the Southern Party, carrying additional food and fuel. From the Southern Party of twelve, a Polar Party of four men, including Scott, would make the final assault on the Pole.

Scott believed the dogs would not be able to climb the uneven surfaces of the Beardmore Glacier. That job would be left to the ponies, which would be used to exhaustion then killed. Their meat would either be eaten immediately or stored for future use. In this way Scott's plan was similar to Amundsen's, if less rigidly scheduled.

Scott grew more anxious as the date of the Pole attempt grew closer. He angrily yelled at Ponting when two crewmen were injured posing for photographs, including one who slipped on an iceberg and received a concussion. Several of the dogs became ill and died of an unknown illness, and the ponies were in poor shape. Despite these setbacks, on October 24 a depot-laying team under the command of Teddy Evans led the two motorized sledges out of camp. On November 1 Scott and his team of twelve left camp with their ponies. Scott could not have left any earlier as ponies required higher temperatures than dogs to travel on the barrier. Not only was Framheim closer to the Pole than Scott's camp, but Amundsen and his dog teams had a two week head start.

By November 5 the engines in both motorized sledges had malfunctioned, and Evans' team resorted to man-hauling to lay the supply depots. The motorized sledges had not even achieved one hundred miles, and were a complete failure. Scott's dog teams did well, but the ponies faltered. Blizzards slowed the team's progress, sometimes to a halt. Whenever a team was stopped by the blizzard, vital food and fuel supplies were used up while no distance south was being covered.

By November 15 Scott's party reached One Ton Depot. Teddy Evans and the now man-hauling Motor Party were still ahead of them, as was Amundsen, who was now over four hundred miles in the lead. On November 21, Scott's team caught up to the Motor Party, who had stopped and were waiting for him. The ponies were weakening rapidly. On November 24 the first one was slaughtered, and others soon followed. Blizzards continued to delay Scott and his men. "What on earth does such weather mean at this time of year?" Scott wrote. "It is more than our share of ill-fortune, I think."

November 24 found Amundsen's Polar Party at the base of the Axel-Heiberg glacier, building a depot and planning their next move. They were already only 340 miles from the Pole. Amundsen decided to take supplies for sixty days and all forty-two remaining dogs up to the Polar Plateau. There his men would kill twenty-four of them, and use eighteen dogs and three sledges to reach the Pole. Six more dogs would then be killed, and the strongest twelve would drag two sledges in the return run to the base of the glacier.

On their first night on the Polar Plateau they carried out the plan. Amundsen turned the portable stove to high pressure, hoping to drown out the sound of gunfire that was soon to follow. "Twenty-four of our brave companions and faithful helpers were marked out for death. It was hard—but it had to be so. We had agreed to shrink from nothing in order to reach our goal. Each man was to kill his own dogs to the number that had been fixed." The nicknamed this camp "The Butcher's Shop."

By December 9, Scott's team was at the base of the 9,000 foot high, one hundred and ten mile long Beardmore Glacier. The last surviving ponies were slaughtered, as Scott did not believe the animals were healthy enough to be of any use on the uphill, high altitude climb. Wilson wrote "Thank God the horses are now all done with and we begin the heavy work ourselves." While the Norwegians viewed the unbelievably grueling work of man-hauling as impractical and inefficient, the British took pride in their ability to do it.

While Scott was first preparing to scale the Beardmore Glacier, Amundsen was already within striking distance of the Pole. He wrote,

> None of us would admit that he was nervous…what would we see when we got there? A vast, endless plain, that no eye had yet seen and no foot yet trodden on; or— No it was an impossibility; with the speed at which we had travelled, we must reach the goal first, there could be no doubt about that. And yet—and yet—wherever there is the smallest loophole, doubt creeps in and gnaws and gnaws and never leaves a poor wretch in peace.

The remaining dogs made the men even more concerned. "What on earth is Uroa scenting?" Bjaaland asked Amundsen, when he observed the dog lifting its head and sniffing due south. Other dogs exhibited the same behavior. Could they smell Scott's Polar Party?

At 3:00 p.m., on December 14, 1911, Amundsen's sledge drivers yelled out "Halt!" Although they could not determine the exact location of the Pole with the instruments they had, "we were so near it that the few miles which possibly separated us from it could not be of the slightest importance," Amundsen wrote.

The team of five men planted the flag together. "This was the only way in which I could show my gratitude to my comrades in this desolate spot," Amundsen wrote. "Five weather-beaten, frost-bitten fists they were that grasped the pole, and raised the waving flag in the air, and planted it first at the geographical South Pole." Further observations over the next few days helped them locate the Pole more accurately, so they travelled to that location. "On December 17 at noon we had completed our observations, and it is certain that we had done all that could be done." A celebratory dinner was held that night, and Bjaaland unveiled a box of cigars he had kept hidden until then. "A cigar at the Pole!" Amundsen exclaimed. "What do you say to that?"

Chapter 13 Leadership Concepts:

The Power of Teamwork: Amundsen's highly skilled, well equipped party showed what can be accomplished by a team operating at top efficiency. They turned what had been a nightmarish struggle for survival for other explorers into a relatively easy attainment of the South Pole.

Remove Divisiveness from the Team: Amundsen quickly banished Johansen from the Polar Party after the veteran explorer confronted him. Although his treatment of Johansen and the others was harsh, once this internal conflict had emerged it had to be dealt with immediately. Amundsen would not allow any discord that would distract the team from their goal.

The Power of Planning: Amundsen's planning was precise, and his methods, though cruel, were creative and remarkably effective. Amundsen used the knowledge he had gathered from the *Belgica* and *Gjoa* journeys, a highly skilled, multitalented crew, and exceptionally detailed preparation to attain his goal. If you can look beyond the Machiavellian deception and ruthlessness, he clearly proved that with proper preparation and planning, the seemingly impossible quickly becomes possible.

Chapter 14

I Wish You a Safe Return

Amundsen was confident that Scott would reach the Pole eventually. "If I know the British rightly, they will never give up once they have started, unless forced by something beyond their control; they are too tough and stubborn for that," he wrote. The Norwegians abandoned some unneeded equipment at the Pole, but they did not cache any food or fuel for Scott's party. Amundsen did leave a letter for Scott, which read "Dear Captain Scott, As you are probably the first to reach this area after us, I will ask you kindly to forward this letter to King Haakon VII. If you can use any of the articles left in the tent please do not hesitate to do so. With kind regards. I wish you a safe return. Yours truly, Roald Amundsen."

On December 23, Scott grew more optimistic as the weather improved, and the team covered twenty-nine miles over the next two days. On Christmas Day, the men enjoyed a special dinner which included plum pudding and cocoa. By New Year's Day they were within 170 miles of the Pole with enough food remaining to reach their goal. Scott now had to decide which men would accompany him on the final push. On the night of January 2, he selected Wilson, Oates, Edgar Evans, and Bowers, for a total of five, a deviation from the original plan of four. Four was the logical number for the Pole Party as each tent had room for four men, and a sledge was more easily pulled by four rather than five. A sketch made by Wilson in November, 1911 shows five men pulling a sledge. It is likely that Wilson drew this as a conceptual model after discussing the possibility with Scott, suggesting that Scott may have been toying with the idea of a five man team weeks earlier.

Bowers was likely chosen for his skill in navigation. Wilson was a natural selection because he was a physician, and because he was Scott's closest friend. Both Wilson and Bowers were also powerful haulers. Teddy Evans and Lashly were likely not selected because they had already man-hauled for over four hundred miles after the motorized sledges had failed, and were therefore underweight and the weakest of the group. Scott was thus left with three men to choose from: Crean, Edgar Evans, and Oates. Both Evans and Oates were strong man-haulers, and Scott decided to take both. Edgar Evans and Oates were chosen over Crean simply because Scott believed he was not quite as powerful a man-hauler as the other two.

The three men not chosen for the final assault were disappointed, but not angry. The selection process for Polar parties was one of the realities of exploration. A few weeks before being chosen, Wilson wrote "whether I shall have the good fortune to be considered strong enough to be one of the final four or not—why, I don't know. No one knows yet who they will be." At the time of their selection, the four men felt lucky to be chosen for the Polar Party.

Scott then gave crucial orders to Teddy Evans to relay to Atkinson at Cape Evans. Scott wanted Meares to travel by dog team, add food and fuel to the supply at Mount Hooper Depot, then continue farther south to meet the returning Polar Party by the middle of February.

In early January, 1912, Lt. Campbell's Northern Party was picked up by the *Terra Nova* from Cape Adare. Since mid-November weak sea ice had prevented the men from sledging away from their base and they had busied themselves with studying and photographing penguins. The ship deposited the Northern Party on a small island near Terra Nova Bay, where they were to spend six weeks geologizing and collecting specimens. Campbell arranged that the *Terra Nova* would retrieve them on or about February 18.

On January 4 Scott's Polar Party set out on the final leg of their journey. The men of the Last Supporting Party cheered and waved goodbye to Scott and his men. It was a touching farewell, but there was a powerful excitement present. At only one hundred and forty five miles from the Pole, the Polar Party could reach the Pole in ten days.

Scott had previously abandoned some equipment, including alpine rope and one set of skis, to reduce the weight of the sledges, so the Polar Party had only four pairs of skis. Bowers was forced to walk, but apparently this was not a hindrance to efficiently pulling the sledge. Bowers wrote that he "connected up to the toggle of the sledge, pulling in the centre between the inner ends of Captain Scott's and Dr. Wilson's traces." Scott wrote that Bowers "has to keep his own pace and luckily does not throw us out at all."

Scott grew concerned that taking a team of five instead of four had been an error, fearing that the additional time needed to cook for five men would cause a significant increase in fuel consumption. At first, an extra half hour was used for the additional necessary cooking, but that time was quickly cut down as the men became used to the routine. Bowers' precise log of camp and meal times provides evidence of this, and indicates that the addition of a fifth man to the team did not adversely impact their chances of survival.

At this point in the journey, food supply was not an issue. On January 7, Scott wrote "Our food continues to amply satisfy. What luck to have hit on such an excellent ration!...We are very comfortable in our double tent...the sleeping-bags remain in good condition...It is quite impossible to speak too highly of my companions." On the same day, however, Wilson's diary entry included an ominous note. "Evans who cut his knuckle some days ago at the last depot...a week ago...has a lot of pus in it tonight."

On January 9, Scott and his team eclipsed the farthest south point that Shackleton had achieved. It had been almost exactly three years since Shackleton was forced to turn his *Nimrod* team around and dash north to avoid starvation. Scott, by contrast, had enough food with him to reach the Pole and return safely to the nearest depot. On January 10 they laid a depot eighty-five miles from the Pole, which lessened their load by almost one hundred pounds. By January 13, they were only fifty-two miles away and closing rapidly on their target. On January 15, they laid a depot during their lunch break, and headed south with food for nine days. In his diary entry for January 16, Wilson wrote "We got away at 8 a.m. and made 7.5 miles by 1:15. Lunched and then in 5.3 miles came on a black flag..."

At 6:30 p.m. on January 17, Scott and his men camped at the South Pole. Despite the many obstacles, they had achieved their objective, but lost the race to Amundsen, who had bested them by a matter of weeks. Wilson wrote "He has beaten us in so far as he made a race of it. We have done what we came for all the same." The final push to the Pole had been accomplished in frigid temperatures, "the coldest march I ever remember," Wilson wrote. "It was difficult to keep one's hands from freezing in double woolen and fur mitts. Oates, Evans and Bowers all have pretty severe frost-bitten noses and cheeks."

"Great God! This is an awful place," Scott wrote in his diary, "and terrible enough for us to have labored to it without the reward of priority." Bowers took pride in the considerable effort the team put forth. In a letter to his mother, he wrote "Here I really am and very glad to be here too. It is a bleak spot—what a place to strive so hard to reach...It is sad that we have been forestalled by the Norwegians, but I am glad that we have done it by good British man-haulage. This is the traditional British sledging method and this is the greatest journey done by man..."

On January 18, Scott and his men planted flags, took pictures, and then started out traveling the eight hundred miles that lay between themselves and safety. Bowers wrote "I am glad to say I am fit and strong...of course none of us are as strong as we were, and one feels inexpressibly weary at the end of a long march if the surface has been heavy. A good meal and a night's rest, however, and you are as fit as ever. Our ration is an excellent one...We have got here and, if ever a journey has been accomplished by honest sweat ours has."

Amundsen and his team had enjoyed a quick and uneventful return journey to Framheim. They averaged over twenty-two miles per day on the trip north, in relatively comfortable temperatures ranging from minus 24 degrees to 23 degrees above. All five men were well. Of the fifty-two dogs that left Framheim in October, eleven returned. Over two years before, in September, 1909, Amundsen had sat in his home on Bundefjord, not far from Christiania, and worked out his scheme to attack the pole. The last sentence of the plan read "Thus we shall be back from the Polar journey on January 25." Amundsen's Polar Party reached Framheim on that very day. The *Fram* departed Antarctica five days later.

Chapter 14 Leadership Concept:

The Power of Effort: Scott's attainment of the Pole was an incredible achievement, especially considering it was done largely through the extremely grueling process of man-hauling. While Amundsen used efficiency, Scott and his men relied on their will. They demonstrated that with extreme effort and perseverance, almost anything can be accomplished. Scott worked as hard as any man on the team, which increased their devotion to him and their commitment to the mission.

Chapter 15

Poor Soldier Nearly Done

By late January Scott, Wilson, Bowers, Oates and Evans were making reasonably good time, but various physical and mental problems were beginning to slow their progress north. Scott recorded on January 23 that Evans, in addition to his frostbite, was "very much annoyed with himself, which is not a good sign." Oates' big toe was turning black, and Wilson was suffering from snow blindness and a deep bruise on his leg that made marching very painful. Soon Evans' fingernails began to fall off, and Scott noted that Evans' "hands are really bad, and to my surprise he shows signs of losing heart over it."

Evans may have been suffering from scurvy, as the men had not eaten meat for more than a month and a half. Evans was something of a finicky eater, and may have purposely avoided meat for a much longer period of time. Geologist Frank Debenham wrote in March 1911, almost a year earlier, that "For supper we had seal liver fried in blubber, excellent. Evans was averse to tasting it as the slightest taste of blubber offends him."

Despite bitter cold, blizzards, the effects of the high altitude of the Polar Plateau, and their assorted physical problems, Scott's team was moving north at a rate that would get them to their various depots, and ultimately to the *Terra Nova*, without starving to death. Although the depots could be difficult to locate, Scott successfully found all of the ones he could reach during the march. By February 4, Scott's team was at the edge of the Beardmore Glacier. They were making good progress, but Oates and Evans were worsening. Oates' toes continued to blacken, and his nose and cheeks had turned yellow. Despite Wilson's best efforts, Evans' fingers were becoming gangrenous.

On February 8, the men found temporary relief from the wind beneath perpendicular sandstone cliffs near Mount Buckley, and made camp. The men spent the afternoon studying rocks, and Wilson discovered coal seams and plant fossils. He excavated thirty-five pounds of rocks with plant imprints, which proved that Antarctica had once enjoyed a tropical climate.

Evans' physical and mental condition continued to worsen. By February 16 he was unable to continue the march. Wilson described him as "sick and giddy and unable to walk even by the sledge or on ski." Scott wrote that Evans "has nearly broken down in the brain we think. He is absolutely changed from his normal self-reliant self." Evans was slowing down the team's advance to a dangerous level. Ten miles from the next depot, and with only enough food rations for one day, they were forced to march ahead as Evans gradually fell further and further behind. When he was nowhere to be seen, they went back for him. Scott wrote "I was the first to reach the poor man and shocked at his appearance; he was on his knees with clothing disarranged, hands uncovered and frostbitten, and a wild look in his eyes. Asked what was the matter, he replied with a slow speech that he did not know."

On the night of February 17, Edgar Evans died. The exact cause of his death was unknown. It may have been the result of scurvy, but Scott and Wilson also recorded that Evans had hit his head on the ice during a fall, and he may have suffered internal bleeding in the brain. Although the remaining four were saddened by Evans' death, it literally saved their lives, at least temporarily. Scott wrote "It is a terrible thing to lose a companion in this way, but calm reflection shows that there could not have been a better ending to the terrible anxieties of the past week...what a desperate pass we were in with a sick man on our hands at such a distance from home." Evans' death also saved Scott from having to make the difficult decision of abandoning him to save the rest of the men. "We have stuck to our sick companions to the last...In the case of Edgar Evans...the safety of the remainder seemed to demand his abandonment, but Providence mercifully removed him at this critical moment."

On February 18 the four remaining members of the Polar Party arrived at Shambles Camp. They loaded their gear onto a sledge that had been left at the camp, and surveyed their situation. They had covered half of their eight hundred mile return journey and had with them eight days of pony meat, one week's food rations for five (now only needed for four), and a sledge in good condition. They were down from the high altitudes of the Plateau and off the difficult surface of the glacier. Three more depots, each containing one week's food supply for five were waiting for them en route to One Ton Depot, which was two hundred and forty miles away. If they could cover a little more than eight and one half miles per day for twenty eight days, they would arrive at One Ton Depot, which literally held over a ton of food, fuel, and gear. It would be a difficult journey, but it could be done.

February 18 had also been the target date for the rescue of the Northern Party. The *Terra Nova* tried to reach the men on three separate occasions, but thick pack ice blocked the ship, and almost trapped her. Finally, the ship sailed to New Zealand, leaving the Northern Party, under the command of Lt. Campbell, to survive on the small piece of rock they dubbed "Inexpressible Island," because they could not find words to describe just how bad conditions there were. With constant gale winds that would often increase to hurricane intensity, the six men of the Northern Party knew their survival was far from guaranteed. Their food was limited to what little rations they had and whatever seals and penguins they could catch. Unlike their months at Cape Adare, when they had lived in the relative comfort of the Southern Cross hut, Inexpressible Island offered them no shelter at all.

On February 19, Tom Crean returned to Hut Point, alone. He reported that The Last Supporting Party had made good time going down the Beardmore Glacier, but then Teddy Evans' health had failed rapidly. Scurvy was the likely cause.

Crean and Lashly had dragged Evans on the sledge for six days, until they reached Corner Camp. There, Lashly stayed with Evans, while Crean walked alone for twenty hours to cover the thirty- five miles to Hut Point.

Atkinson had planned to travel south with dog teams on February 20th to aid the returning Polar Party, but Crean's news of Teddy Evans' condition changed Atkinson's mind. His top priority became keeping Teddy Evans alive. Evans and Lashly were rescued by Atkinson and Gerof and brought back to Hut Point. Evans conveyed Scott's last orders to Atkinson, which stated that Meares should drive the dog teams out to meet them at a point past the Mount Hooper Depot.

The *Terra Nova* was due to arrive at Cape Evans in late February, delivering new dogs for a second Pole attempt if needed, and picking up men who were leaving the expedition rather than staying on for a second winter. Among the men planning to leave was Meares. With Atkinson, the only physician available, tending to Evans, and Meares about to leave, the task of taking the dog teams to meet Scott fell to Cherry-Garrard, who left with Gerof on February 25. Days later, Teddy Evans, Meares, and several other crewmen left Antarctica aboard the *Terra Nova*.

The men of Scott's Polar Party had experienced difficult days since leaving Shambles Camp. Rough surface conditions had slowed them, and at the first depot they reached they were surprised to find that cans of vital fuel were partially empty. The cans used metal tops, twisted on over leather washers. This was an upgrade over the system used during Scott's first expedition aboard the *Discovery*, when cork was used to close the containers. The cans with cork had often leaked when tipped on the sledge, but Scott could not account for the loss of fuel from the new cans.

The red fuel containers had been placed on top of the depots to make the supply mounds more visible. It is likely that exposure to the sun during the day and bitter cold at night caused temperature changes that cracked the leather washers, which allowed for evaporation of the precious fuel. Had the fuel cans been packed within the depot among the other supplies, they would have been out of the sun, not exposed to extreme temperature changes, and the cracking and evaporation might not have occurred.

On February 25, the day that Cherry-Garrard and Gerof left with the dog teams, the temperature on the Barrier began to plummet, and it became unseasonably cold, even for Antarctica. On the last day of February, Scott recorded a nighttime temperature of minus forty-one. On March 2, Oates revealed that his feet were badly frostbitten. Each morning it would take him over an hour to put on his boots, delaying the beginning of the day's march. On March 3, the men traveled ten miles, then nine the following day, with Oates marching forward in incredible pain. Worst of all, the bitterly cold temperatures also crystallized the surface, making it much more difficult to pull the sledge.

Scott had based his expedition plan on the weather chart of Simpson, the expedition meteorologist. Scott reasonably expected warmer weather on the Barrier in late February and early March. Along with the unusually cold weather, there was a strange absence of the wind from the south. During Shackleton's *Nimrod* expedition, a sail mounted on the sledge helped propel the men north. The sledge sail was of no use to Scott, Wilson, Bowers and Oates.

Cherry-Garrard and Gerof reached One Ton Depot in the late hours of March 3, and there they waited for Scott and his men, who unbeknownst to Cherry-Garrard, were only one hundred miles to the south at the time. Oates' condition was worsening. "Poor Soldier nearly done," Scott wrote. "It is pathetic enough because we can do nothing for him…none of us expected these terribly low temperatures." By March 6 they were within eighty miles of One Ton Depot. Oates continued to help drag the sledge, in spite of his condition. Scott wrote, "If we were all fit I should have hopes of getting through, but the poor Soldier has become a terrible hindrance, though he does his utmost and suffers much." On March 7, while Scott and his men struggled desperately for survival, Roald Amundsen cabled news of his historic accomplishment to Norway, England, and the rest of the world.

March 10 was a crucial day. Scott, Bowers, Wilson and Oates reached Mount Hooper Depot, the last depot before One

Ton, and the place where Scott had instructed Teddy Evans to have Meares restock, and then continue south to meet the returning Polar Party in early March. It was obvious that neither Meares nor anyone else had been to Mount Hooper Depot to add provisions. Worse, the amount of food and fuel were less than even a normal depot would hold. Scott wrote "I don't know that anyone is to blame. The dogs which would have been our salvation have evidently failed. Meares had a bad trip home I suppose…It's a miserable jumble."

Also on March 10, Cherry-Garrard and Gerof, with no sign of Scott or his men, turned north from One Ton Depot and began their journey back to their base at Camp Evans. Scott, Oates, Wilson and Bowers were only sixty miles away. Cherry-Garrard had not ventured south of One Ton Depot since their arrival six days earlier, and later defended his actions: "Since there was no depot of dog-food at One Ton is was not possible to go farther South without killing dogs. My orders on this point were perfectly explicit; I saw no reason for disobeying them…I had no reason to suspect that the Polar Party could be in want of food…Thus I felt little anxiety for the Polar Party."

A blizzard on the 10th trapped the remaining four men of the Polar Party in their tent. Scott wrote "Titus Oates is very near the end, one feels. What we or he will do, God only knows. We discussed the matter after breakfast; he is a brave fine fellow and understands the situation, but he practically asked for advice. Nothing could be said but to urge him to march as long as he could." On March 11, Scott "practically ordered Wilson to hand over the means of ending our troubles (opium tablets Wilson kept in his medical case) to us, so that anyone of us may know how to do so." By March 12, Oates could no longer use his fingers, and would have been unable to take the tablets without assistance.

By March 17, Oates no longer had the strength to travel. Scott, Wilson, and Bowers would not consider leaving him behind, but he refused to be a hindrance to the team. Scott wrote "Oates said he couldn't go on; he proposed we should leave him in his sleeping bag. That we could not do, and we induced him to come on…he struggled on and we made a few miles. At night he was worse and we knew the end had come…He slept through the night before last, hoping not to wake; but he woke in the morning—yesterday. It was blowing a blizzard. He said, 'I am just going outside and may be some time.' He went out into the blizzard and we have not seen him since...We knew that poor Oates was walking to his death, but though we tried to dissuade him, we knew it was the act of a brave man and an English gentleman. We all hope to meet the end with a similar spirit, and assuredly the end is not far." Oates never returned, and his body has never been found. His heroic act of selflessness eventually made him a legendary figure in British history and Polar exploration. The "Soldier" died on his birthday. He was thirty-two years old.

Scott, Wilson and Bowers resumed the march and two days later were only eleven miles south of One Ton Depot and salvation. Scott was suffering from severe frostbite on his right foot and could barely walk. Even worse, their food supply was gone. Wilson and Bowers planned to trek to One Ton Depot, then return to rescue Scott. Bowers penned a letter to his mother, which stated "I am still strong and hope to reach [One Ton Depot] with Dr. Wilson and get the food and fuel necessary for our lives. God alone knows what will be the outcome of the 22 miles march...There will be no shame however and you will know that I have struggled to the end." Wilson wrote to his wife Oriana "Birdie and I are going to try and reach the Depot 11 miles north of us and return to this tent where Captain Scott is lying with a frozen foot...I shall simply fall and go to sleep in the snow...We have struggled to the end and we have nothing to regret...The Barrier has beaten us—though we got to the Pole."

With luck they might have made it, but luck was not on their side. A powerful blizzard struck, making travel impossible. Scott wrote letters to Wilson's wife and Bowers' mother, praising their efforts and sacrifice. He wrote to his own mother and to Kathleen, leaving instructions for her to raise their son with an interest in "natural history," and to remarry, so she could be her "happy self again." Scott's final notation, "For God's sake look after our people," reflected his concern for the families of the men who had given their lives under his command.

For the six men of the Northern Party on Inexpressible Island, daily life was a constant struggle for survival. They had created a shelter by tunneling into the biggest snow drift they could find. Remarkably, they were able to construct an eight foot by twelve foot cave, but only five and a half feet high at its tallest point. A blubber stove provided the only light, some desperately needed heat and allowed them to cook, but poor ventilation kept the air filled with an oily brown smoke. Though cramped and dark, the cave kept the men of the Northern Party sheltered from the vicious, unremitting winds of Inexpressible Island. To make matters worse, in late April, the Sun disappeared.

They often dreamt of the *Terra Nova*, as if those on the ship were attempting to contact them. As time went on, their sleep was filled with nightmarish images of catastrophes involving the Southern Party, or of the *Terra Nova* sailing away from them to New Zealand. As rations grew dangerously low in early July, their dreams focused solely on food.

When two seals appeared, Campbell and Petty Officer George Abbot set after them, and the seals scurried for the water. Without these two animals, it was likely the men of the Northern Party would not survive the winter. Campbell and Abbot fought desperately with knives and ice axes to subdue the seals. Although they were successful, Abbot cut his hand in the fight. His severed tendons were irreparably damaged, and he permanently lost the ability to bend three of his fingers.

Campbell did his best to keep the men optimistic and alive. Saturday evenings were filled with songs, and on Sunday mornings they said psalms, sang hymns, and Campbell read from the New Testament. During the week they read aloud from the three books they had with them: *Life of Stevenson*, *Simon the Jester*, and *David Copperfield*. On Sundays each man enjoyed one and a half ounces of chocolate and tea with sugar.

On August 13, the Sun reappeared, and the men of the Northern Party began to emerge from their cave. Unsure if a rescue ship would ever arrive, they decided to sledge the two hundred and fifty miles back to Cape Evans. They left Inexpressible Island for good on September 30, and when they sighted Mount Erebus on October 10, they knew they were close.

For the men at Cape Evans, the darkness of April had made it impossible to send out a search party to look for the bodies of the Polar Party. In late October a team was dispatched, and on November 12, 1912, Wright, the young physicist, spotted the tent among the endless white expanse. Drifting snow had almost completely covered the canvas, and only the tip was exposed. After the snow was carefully dug away, Atkinson and Lashly went inside and discovered the bodies. Wilson and Bowers had died in their sleeping bags. Scott had pushed aside the flaps of his sleeping bag, and his hand lay on Wilson, his devoted friend.

Diaries, letters, and other effects were removed, as were the rocks that Wilson had taken from Mt. Buckley. The diaries soon revealed the fate of Evans and Oates. The tent poles were removed, allowing it to fall over the bodies, and a cairn of snow was built over the tent, with a cross made of skis on the top. A search for Oates' body turned up only his sleeping bag and personal effects, and a cairn was built to honor the fallen soldier. In a powerfully symbolic gesture, Gran, the only Norwegian member of the *Terra Nova* expedition, used Scott's skis on the return trip to Cape Evans, to make sure that the skis completed their journey.

The search team received some badly needed good news when they returned to Hut Point and learned that the entire Northern Party had arrived safely on November 6. Priestley noted that the men of the Northern Party owed an enormous debt to their leader, Lt. Campbell, for his optimism and resourcefulness.

The *Terra Nova*, under the command of Teddy Evans, returned to Cape Evans in January, 1913, picked up its crew and left Antarctica, leaving behind the bodies of Robert Scott, Edward Wilson, Birdie Bowers, Edgar Evans, and Titus Oates. On January 9, Hjalmar Johansen, survivor of Nansen's North Pole attempt and disgraced crewmember of Amundsen's South Pole expedition, committed suicide in Oslo.

Chapter 15 Leadership Concept:

The Power of Optimism: The unheralded Campbell accomplished a remarkable feat of leadership by keeping the men of the Northern Party alive during a terrible winter on Inexpressible Island. He kept his men mentally healthy through stories, songs, routine, and an optimistic outlook that inspired the men to fight for their survival.

Chapter 16

Penguin Egg Omelets

Certain expeditions highlight the constant danger inherent in Antarctic exploration, and the perseverance needed to survive under the most difficult conditions. The Australasian Antarctic Expedition, led by Douglas Mawson, the brilliant Australian scientist who had climbed Mount Erebus and found the South Magnetic Pole serving under Shackleton on the *Nimrod*, is one such story.

The *Aurora* arrived at Commonwealth Bay, near Adelie Land in East Antarctica on January 8, 1912. After Captain John King Davis deposited Mawson and other crewmembers at Cape Denison, the *Aurora* sailed west to disembark a party commanded by Frank Wild, now on his third Antarctic expedition. Mawson had developed an elaborate plan that involved several teams simultaneously exploring and mapping areas of East Antarctica south of Australia.

Though a hut was built at Cape Denison, the men soon realized that another shelter would be needed, as the cape was home to a seemingly endless blizzard blowing down from the Polar Plateau. In August, a large cavern was carved into the ice about five miles from the hut. Once inside "Aladdin's Cave," as they called their new home, the blizzard was silenced.

On November 10, 1912 Mawson was about to lead his team out of camp. Mawson's party consisted of Xavier Mertz,

28, a champion skier and expert mountaineer from Switzerland, and Belgrave Ninnis, 23, a Lieutenant in the British Army. Ninnis, assisted by his close friend Mertz, was in charge of the expedition's dogs. Mertz was known for his cooking, and on this morning the men of Cape Denison clamored around the stove waiting for his specialty, penguin egg omelets.

Two days after Mawson, Mertz and Ninnis left camp, Atkinson, Cherry-Garrard and the rest of the *Terra Nova's* search team found the bodies of Scott, Wilson, and Bowers eleven miles south of One Ton Depot. Years earlier, Scott had asked Mawson to join his expedition and be part of his Polar Party, but Mawson had declined, as his interest lay purely in scientific discovery, and not with attainment of the Pole.

Mawson's team, using dogs to pull their sledges, made good time, but soon the hazards of Antarctic travel became dramatically evident. On November 20, the leading dogs of Mawson's sledge fell into a crevasse and dangled in their harnesses, but the sledge stayed on the surface and the animals were quickly pulled to safety. The following day, while Mertz cooked lunch, Mawson and Ninnis left camp to photograph a blue abyss. Ninnis fell through a lid of frozen drift, the type that covers many crevasses and makes them virtually undetectable. With Ninnis's head and arms still above the surface, Mawson was able to haul his friend out. Mawson looked into the hole, and saw nothing but darkness.

On December 6 a blizzard confined the three men to their tent. They were forced to stay in their sleeping bags to keep warm, and while they were grateful for the rest, by the third day they had grown quite bored. Mertz, having already finished his copy of *Sherlock Holmes*, quoted sections from memory for everyone's amusement.

On the morning of December 14, Mertz skied far in the lead while Mawson and Ninnis trailed on sledges pulled by dogs. The sun was shining and the men were happy. Mertz even sang to himself as he skied, but suddenly Mawson noticed that Mertz had stopped and was holding up his ski pole, a clear warning. It took a few minutes for Mawson to reach the area on his sledge, but he saw nothing unusual. There was a possible crevasse beneath his sledge, but Mawson did not view it as particularly dangerous. He yelled a warning to Ninnis, who was walking next to his own sledge. Ninnis heeded the warning by changing the direction of his team.

Soon after, Mawson noticed Mertz had again halted, and was peering anxiously in his direction. Mawson turned, but saw nothing behind him but his own tracks. Ninnis and his sledge were gone. Mawson raced back to find an eleven foot wide hole in the ice. Mertz and Mawson peered over and shouted into the crevasse. They could see a gravely injured dog, their tent, and a container of food on a ledge one hundred and fifty feet down, but beyond the ledge was darkness.

They called to Ninnis for three hours without a reply. With insufficient rope to reach the ledge, the men had to abandon the dogs, their supplies, and any hope of finding their friend. Mawson and Mertz now found themselves in a desperate position. The loss of Ninnis' sledge meant more than the terrible passing of their friend and companion. Most of their food, the six strongest dogs and all of the dog food were gone. They would now have to travel three hundred miles to reach the Cape Denison Hut with six weak dogs and food for only ten days.

Ironically, the best dogs and most of the food had been placed on the trailing sledge because it was thought that if a sledge were to break through a crevasse lid it would more likely be the first one. Why had Mawson's sledge passed over the crevasse safely while Ninnis' had not? Mawson had been sitting on his sledge when it crossed the crevasse lid, while Ninnis had been walking next to his. Mawson believed that the concentrated weight of one of Ninnis' steps was enough to break the lid.

Mawson and Mertz soon began killing some of the dogs to provide food for the other dogs and themselves. Despite eating the dog meat, the men were still living on a starvation diet, and tried to keep the thought of food from entering their minds. On December 17, when the faithful dog Johnson became too fatigued to continue, they put him on the sledge and dragged him along. By camp that night Johnson was unable to stand or eat his food, and was killed.

By December 30, sixteen days since the terrible death of Ninnis, things were finally looking up for Mertz and Mawson.

The surface flattened, allowing for much easier and faster travel. Their spirits improved, and Mawson believed that their fortunes had changed. Fate, however, had decreed that Mawson would have to finish this journey alone.

Mertz soon became depressed, a radical transformation from his usual cheerful demeanor, and displayed symptoms of dysentery. He rapidly disintegrated physically and mentally. Although he had shown tremendous resistance to cold in the past, frostbite now set in. A disoriented Mertz refused to believe he had frostbite on his fingers, and actually bit off a piece of one of them.

Mawson did his best to lessen Mertz' suffering and keep him optimistic. They talked about getting back to the *Aurora*, and agreed that once on board Mertz would stir up his delicious penguin egg omelets. On the morning of January 7, however, Mertz began to rant incoherently, and although he improved somewhat in the afternoon, he died that night. Mawson was crushed. He toggled Mertz up in his sleeping bag, and lay next to him for the rest of the night.

Alone in the Antarctic, Douglas Mawson now began a one hundred mile journey of survival. He was determined, but suffered terribly. His fingers and nose were horribly frostbitten, and he endured painful snow-blindness. On January 11, Mawson discovered that the soles of his feet were being held on merely by his socks.

On January 17, Mawson fell into a crevasse, suspended only by the harness rope from the sledge, which had remained on the surface. Weak from starvation, it was grueling for Mawson to climb back to the surface, but he managed to reach the top with tremendous effort. Just as he attempted to crawl from the overhanging crevasse lid onto the ice, the lid gave way and he fell again into the abyss.

He hung from the rope, exhausted, slowly spinning as the rope twisted back and forth. He considered freeing himself from the harness and plunging to his death—the release from suffering and the excitement of seeing what lay beyond suddenly seemed very appealing. Suicidal thoughts soon left Mawson's mind, however, and he made one last effort for his life. Again he climbed the rope, but this time threw his feet up first onto the crevasse lid, and slid to safety on solid ice. He drifted into unconsciousness as snow fell upon him.

As Mawson continued his journey, the weather grew significantly worse. A large snowstorm on January 25 almost buried him alive as he lay in his sleeping bag inside his tent. After much exertion he freed himself, but with only five pounds of food left and his physical condition worsening, his chances of survival were not high.

On the evening of January 28 the weather improved. Mawson started his journey on the morning of the 29th dragging his sledge, pondering if the remaining two pounds of dog meat, raisins and chocolate would last long enough to reach the hut at Cape Denison. Suddenly he spotted something dark through the haze. It was a bag of food on top of a cairn built by a rescue party that included expedition photographer Frank Hurley and chief medical officer Archibald McLean. A note provided Mawson with a great deal of information. He had just missed the rescue party, who had left the cairn only six hours earlier, but Aladdin's Cave was only 23 miles away, and the ship was waiting at the hut. Also, Amundsen had reached the Pole, while Scott was staying another year in Antarctica. News of Scott's death had not yet reached the men of the *Aurora*.

With a renewed energy, Mawson took up the trek again, and despite blizzard conditions he reached Aladdin's Cave on February 1. The blizzard continued for a week, trapping Mawson in the cave. On February 8 the wind finally lessened and Mawson left the safety of the cave in search of the hut and the *Aurora*. As Mawson drew closer to the coast, he spied the ship in the distance, sailing away. As he approached the harbor, however, he saw men. Five members of the crew had stayed behind to search for Mawson's party.

As wireless radio was now operational at the hut and on the ship, Mawson recalled the *Aurora*, but the weather made it impossible for the vessel to reach them. The *Aurora* sailed west to pick up Frank Wild's party, and returned them to Hobart in March. Mawson and his men were finally retrieved in December and returned to cheering crowds in Adelaide, Australia in late February 1914. Mawson would not return to the Antarctic until 1929, but the *Aurora* would embark on another ill-fated mission before the year was out.

Chapter 16 Leadership Concept:

The Power of Perseverance: Mawson's story, besides graphically depicting the perils of Antarctic exploration, rivals any tale of perseverance. Mawson demonstrated what can be accomplished through tenacious effort and the will to survive. When leaders in more mundane situations face serious problems or tough choices, they would be wise to think of Mawson, who literally pulled himself out of the abyss.

Chapter 17

The First to be Eaten

On July 16, 1910, Scott had arrived at Waterloo train station for the first step of his fateful journey. Shackleton attended the sendoff, and prompted the crowd for "Three cheers for Captain Scott!" From there Scott took the train to Southampton, then sailed south and rendezvoused with the *Terra Nova*, which had left England in June.

Also in attendance at Waterloo Station that day was Dr. Wilhelm Filchner, a German officer who was planning to lead his own Antarctic expedition. Filchner planned to sail into the Weddell Sea, traverse Antarctica, then be picked up near the Ross Sea, possibly meeting up with Scott's men at the Ross Sea base at McMurdo Sound. Filchner purchased a ship and sailed with six members of his expedition to Spitsbergen, a Norwegian island in the Arctic Ocean, to practice in polar environments. Their training completed, they sailed south, and in December, 1911 left South Georgia Island aboard the *Deutschland* bound for Antarctica.

Shackleton, meanwhile, was dreaming of returning south himself. In January of 1912, unaware that the South Pole had already been reached, he wrote to a friend "I wish I could get another Expedition, and be away from all business worries. All the troubles of the South are nothing compared to day after day of business." Since his last trip to the Antarctic, Shackleton had been involved in various failed business ventures, including poorly advised investments in Hungarian mines.

The next several months were tumultuous for Shackleton. When news of Amundsen's attainment of the South Pole reached England in March, Shackleton's hopes were dashed. On April 15, the *Titanic* sank in the North Atlantic after colliding with an iceberg. Shackleton was called to provide expert testimony at the official hearings on the disaster. He criticized the speed of the ship as being excessive for navigating through waters with known icebergs. He also suggested that the Captain was likely influenced by the presence of the ship's owners. "When the owner is on board, you go," Shackleton stated.

In January, 1913, Filchner returned from Antarctica and docked in Buenos Aires. The *Deutschland* expedition had failed. Filchner had been unable to move inland from the coast near the Weddell Sea. In February, the *Terra Nova* arrived in New Zealand, and the world first learned that Scott, Wilson and the other three members of the Polar Party had died returning from the South Pole. Shackleton was now the only surviving member of the trio that had pushed so far south during the *Discovery* expedition.

Being the first man to the South Pole was no longer an obtainable goal for Shackleton. Filchner's scheme, however, seemed viable, and Shackleton soon forged a similar version of his own. He would land a party at a base near the Weddell Sea and lead a team that would travel across the continent, pass directly through the South Pole and continue on to the opposite coast. A second ship would sail into the Ross Sea and send men and dogs inland to lay depots of food and supplies for Shackleton and his men to use on the outbound leg of their journey. The second ship would eventually transport Shackleton's expedition team and the depot laying parties back to New Zealand. Shackleton began the familiar task of raising capital. Using his fame and personal charm he secured funding, and by the summer of 1914 preparations for the Imperial Trans-Antarctic Expedition were nearing completion.

Shackleton carefully selected the crew of the *Endurance*, the ship that would carry him into the Weddell Sea.

Frank Wild, who had accompanied Shackleton during their attempt to reach the South Pole during the *Nimrod* expedition, was chosen as Second in Command. It was Wild's job to sort through the five *thousand* applications Shackleton received for crew positions. Wild separated candidates into three categories: "Mad," "Hopeless," and "Possible." Shackleton examined the "Possible" list, narrowed it to a small pool that he would personally interview, and ultimately compiled a diverse crew with a combination of scientific and maritime skills.

Frank Worsley was selected as Captain. Worsley's presence on the *Endurance* was the result of an odd dream, in which he saw himself navigating a boat down an ice covered Burlington Street in London. Like many sailors, Worsley was superstitious, and the next morning he promptly went to Burlington Street, where he happened upon a door with a sign that read "Imperial Trans-Antarctic Expedition." Shackleton took an instant liking to him, and signed Worsley on.

Close friends Tom Crean and Alf Cheetham anchored a team of veteran sailors. Crean had served on both of Scott's expeditions, and had distinguished himself as a member of the *Terra Nova* when he walked alone for thirty-five miles across the Ross Ice Shelf to get help when Teddy Evans grew too weak to travel. Cheetham had served on the *Morning*, relief ship of the *Discovery*, and on both the *Nimrod* and the *Terra Nova*. At 47, Cheetham had spent more time below the Antarctic Circle than any other sailor or explorer.

Two physicians, Alexander Macklin and James McIlroy were selected, along with a team of scientists. Scotsman James Wordie was named expedition geologist and placed in charge of the scientific staff. Meteorologist Leonard Hussey brought his banjo, which would later prove an important source of entertainment. The crew also included an artist, George Marston, and Australian Frank Hurley, expedition photographer. Shackleton informed all crew members that they would be expected to do any and all tasks required during the voyage. Scientists and sailors alike would share equally in the difficult work ahead.

On June 28, 1914 Archduke Ferdinand of Austria, first in line to the Austro-Hungarian throne, was murdered by a Serb nationalist. The assassination sparked World War I, and by August Britain was on the verge of war. Shackleton contacted the Admiralty, and volunteered to cancel the expedition immediately and return the ship, stores, and crew to the war effort. Shackleton received a prompt reply from Winston Churchill, First Lord of the Admiralty, in the form of a telegram which read simply "Proceed."

While the war began in Europe, Worsley and the crew of the *Endurance* sailed south, stopping in Buenos Aires, where Shackleton was due to meet them, and took on additional crewmen. Perce Blackborrow, a nineteen year old Welsh seaman, asked to join the expedition, but was not accepted. Undeterred, Blackborrow stowed himself away and was only discovered days later when the *Endurance* was already on the ocean. Shackleton told Blackborrow that he would be taken off the ship at the next stop and sent back to Buenos Aires. When Blackborrow protested, Shackleton said "Do you know on these expeditions, we often get very hungry, and if there is a stowaway available, he is the first to be eaten?" Blackborrow replied "They'd get a lot more meat off you, sir!" Shackleton assigned Blackborrow to be the cook's assistant.

Endurance's final stop before heading to Antarctica was South Georgia Island, home of the Norwegian whaling station Stromness. The crew spent a month in South Georgia, waiting for ice in the Weddell Sea to break up, and a strong bond of friendship developed between the explorers and the whalers. Finally, on December 5, 1914, the *Endurance* left port for the last time.

On January 2, 1915, the *Endurance* covered 124 miles and was making excellent progress south. Soon, however, the ship entered pack ice in the Weddell Sea, and by January 19, she was stuck. On February 14 there was hope for an escape when a lead (a break in the ice) emerged just three hundred yards from the ship. A tremendous effort was made to free the *Endurance* using saws, boathooks, poles, and the ship's engines, but after two days Shackleton, Wild and Worsley concluded it would be impossible to break the grip of the ice. A wave of depression began to overtake the crew, but Shackleton worked quickly to improve the men's morale. He arranged for a soccer game on the ice, which the crew greatly enjoyed.

In an effort to keep spirits up, Shackleton created routines, rearranged sleeping quarters, and started speaking to crewmembers in small groups. Besides meeting with the men personally, he also made sure that his policy of equal treatment was evident. Although he was the leader of the expedition and a legend in the field of exploration, Shackleton lived the same as any other crew member. He shared his tent as the other men did, ate the same rations, and did equal work. He sacrificed his best pair of boots to a sailor who needed them, and his selflessness and positive attitude engendered a deep loyalty among his crew.

Shackleton planned to wait out the Antarctic winter, which would be at its height in July and August, then resume sailing towards the coast in the spring when warmer temperatures broke up the ice. As time passed, however, Shackleton realized the ship would not survive the winter. He saw no reason to prematurely upset the crew, so he confided this information only to Wild and Worsley. Shackleton told his Captain "You had better make up your mind that it is only a matter of time...Wild and I know how you feel about the *Endurance*, but what the ice gets, the ice keeps." Wild added "We are not going to let the ice get us."

Shackleton worked tirelessly to keep the men occupied and upbeat. He organized soccer games, sled dog races, and various forms of nightly entertainment including card games, comedy skits, plays, singing contests, and lectures. In June, five months after the *Endurance* had become trapped, the men were still in good spirits due to Shackleton's genius for keeping up morale.

By August the crew of the Imperial Trans-Antarctic Expedition were far from where they had planned to be when their journey began. Shackleton's men were comfortable enough, living in the *Endurance* and exercising on the ice, but the ship was slowly being crushed, and soon the crew would be castaways on the frozen Weddell Sea. As currents and winds from the Southern Ocean pushed the pack ice up against the immovable coast, the ship was caught in a vice. The pressure lifted the *Endurance* up and out of the ice, tossing it over on its side. Although the ship later righted itself, the power of the ice was too strong, and slowly she began to break apart. Preparations were made to abandon the vessel. The men unloaded what they could, including the dogs, supplies, sledges, fuel and food. On October 24 the ice tore a hole in the ship, and it quickly flooded. Within three days the *Endurance* was destroyed.

The men waited for Shackleton's orders. The "Boss," as he was affectionately referred to by the crew, kept his remarks concise. Survival was within their reach. They could get to land, and safety, if they worked hard and cooperated with each other. Almost immediately the spirits of the men improved, and they began to laugh, joke, and encourage each other. They trusted Shackleton to see them through.

The *Endurance* did not sink all at once. The men watched it gradually break apart as parts of the ship disappeared under the ice. An electric light, powered by a small battery, stayed lit during the ship's last moments. Right before dawn, as the final beam of the *Endurance* snapped, the light flickered and went dark.

Shackleton realized the importance of keeping the crew focused on a plan of action. Although they no longer had their ship, they had three small lifeboats that could provide their salvation. Three hundred and fifty miles away lay Paulet Island, which Shackleton knew held a store of clothing, fuel, and food. The strategy was simple but challenging. With the help of their sled dogs, the men would drag the lifeboats and sledges, packed with supplies, over the ice until they reached water. From there they would use the lifeboats to reach Paulet Island.

Successful sledge travel demanded economy of weight. Shackleton allowed each man to carry only two pounds of gear, excluding sleeping bags. Naturally this led to difficult decisions about which personal items to keep. Shackleton went first, and in front of the crew discarded coins, a cigarette case, and a watch, all made of gold. Frank Hurley, the expedition's photographer, worked with Shackleton to decide which heavy plate glass negatives he would take with him, and which ones to abandon. Shackleton had Hurley smash the discarded ones to remove the temptation to return for them.

While dog teams pulled seven smaller sledges loaded with supplies, the men dragged the three boats on larger sledges, but any advance soon proved impossible. The ice was not an even, smooth surface, but instead a series of ridges, pushed up by the same pressure that had stove the *Endurance*. To make matters worse, during midday the sun began to melt the snow that lay on top of the ice, creating a mushy mixture that was hard to walk on. After only one half mile it was clear that even the larger sledges could not bear the weight of the boats. Shackleton decided to strengthen the sledges with wood from the *Endurance*. The wreck was now highly unstable, partly submerged, and being held up only by ice which could shift at any time. At great risk and working in freezing water, the men used crowbars and axes to extract whatever useful materials they could.

Even with the reinforced sledges, further attempts at dragging the boats proved equally futile. On November 1 Shackleton abandoned the march and quickly came up with a new strategy. The men would establish camp on the ice, and let the winds and currents slowly bring the floes closer to land. Ocean Camp, as it came to be called, was set up. The men lived in tents, slept in sleeping bags, and tried to fight off boredom. On November 21, 1915, the *Endurance* finally lost her battle with the ice and sunk. The crew watched the ship go under. For a moment, a small space remained where the ship had been, but then the ice closed and the *Endurance* was gone. The next day, Shackleton commemorated the ship by planting the Union Jack that had been presented to him by the King. This simple act of rebellion against the ice raised the spirits of the entire crew.

Chapter 17 Leadership Concepts:

Equal Treatment and Sacrifice: Shackleton made sure that his policy of equal treatment was evident. He ate the same food, lived in the same tents, and gave his boots to a man who needed them. This egalitarianism went a long way towards earning the trust and respect of the crew.

Selective Disbursement of Information: When Shackleton realized the *Endurance* would not survive, he shared this information only with Wild and Worsley, realizing that there was no need to alarm the crew prematurely. By doing this Shackleton was able to keep the men happier for a longer period of time, and not worry them over something they had no control over.

Chapter 18

All Mothers Will Understand

As the weeks at Ocean Camp dragged on, there was little to do. Occasionally parties would leave the camp to hunt seal and penguin, but otherwise the men were bored and restless. Cliques developed, nerves frayed and tempers were short. Shackleton, a keen judge of people, used tact, diplomacy and creativity to end the negativity and make sure the men got along well with each other. He arranged tent assignments carefully, considering the personalities involved. The Boss recognized that one despondent individual or small group could impact the morale of the entire crew. When necessary, he would change assignments on a pretext, often bringing the unhappiest men into his own tent where he could keep a careful watch over them and improve their spirits. Shackleton would often remind the men that unity was the key to their strength.

By late December, after eight long weeks at Ocean Camp, the situation was beginning to change. Blizzards had swept the floe over one hundred miles, but the fierce winds had also damaged the ice, making it increasingly unstable. The warmer weather of summer brought the relief of more sunlight and fewer blizzards, but now the men would sink when they walked in the soft snow. At night, the snow melted under their sleeping bags and in the morning they would find themselves in small pools of water.

As Christmas approached, Shackleton ordered that a special meal of saved rations, including ham, peaches, and sausages be served. The following day, the crew resumed their march towards the ocean. Shackleton decided to drag only two boats, the *James Caird* and the *Dudley Docker*, leaving the *Stancomb Wills* behind. In the stern of the *Stancomb Wills*, Worsley left a bottle with a message inside, which read in part "*Endurance* crushed and abandoned...All hands to-morrow proceeding to the westward. All well. December 23rd, 1915. E.H. Shackleton."

Marching conditions had changed very little since their first attempt. Shackleton and Wild walked ahead of the men, trying to chip away the sharp points of ice and clear a path for the sledges. Since each boat weighed almost a ton, it could only be dragged if all the men pulled, so they began the tedious process of relaying. They would drag one boat, march back to the other and drag that one forward. They were traveling three miles, two of which involved heavy pulling, for every one mile gained. It was easier to drag when the snow was firmer, so after one day Shackleton revised his plan and had the men sleep during the day and haul the boats at night.

On December 27, Chippy McNeish, the carpenter, openly rebelled against the tortuous relaying. Shackleton responded quickly to McNeish's comments. Ship's articles, which stipulated the duties of the crew (even after the loss of the ship) were read to the men. McNeish fell back in line, and the dragging resumed.

Ultimately, McNeish may have been right, even if he had picked a poor way to voice his disagreement. After a week of what Wild called "the hardest imaginable labour" they had covered only seven miles, and further marching was clearly pointless. In addition to being exhausting and unproductive, the journey had been dangerous. Crean had almost died after plunging through thin ice into freezing water.

Shackleton abandoned the plan to drag the boats across the ice. Instead, the crew established the aptly named Patience Camp on the largest ice floe they could find. There they would wait for the ice to slowly drift towards land, and when they were close enough they would take to their boats and row.

As New Year's Day 1916 arrived the men of the *Endurance* had been below the Antarctic Circle for exactly one year. Every day hunting parties would search for penguins and seals, with varying degrees of success. In mid-January Hurley and Macklin had taken empty sledges and dog teams to the deserted Ocean Camp and brought back food that had been left there, including cereals, jam, dry milk and potted meats. In addition to their stores, the men killed penguins, seals and sea leopards for food and fuel. On one occasion, the contents of a sea leopard's stomach provided sixty fresh, undigested fish. Considerable pains were taken to vary the menu and prevent the tedium of eating the same food every day.

Despite the crew's efforts the food supply began to run dangerously low. Rations were reduced and it eventually became necessary to slaughter the dogs, as there was not enough food for the animals and the men. "Shackleton ordered the dogs to be shot," Wild recorded. "This duty fell upon me and was the worst job I ever had in my life; I have known many men I would rather shoot than the worst of the dogs."

On February 28 Worsley urged Shackleton to use the time at Patience Camp to retrieve the third boat, the *Stancomb Wills*, from Ocean Camp. Though it took some persuading, Shackleton ultimately agreed. It would prove to be a very good decision.

Shackleton was intensely focused on keeping the men alive, in good spirits, and ultimately getting them to safety. Wild remembered that "practically the whole of March was stormy and miserable...During this period Shackleton had a severe attack of sciatica and for several days could not leave his sleeping bag without assistance. This was the only time whilst we were on the floe that he failed to visit each tent, even during blizzards, and make enquiries as to every man's health and comfort."

Shackleton had never lost a man under his command, as the crew was well aware. Patience Camp, however, was slowly moving towards a very dangerous end, when the ice would reach warmer waters and suddenly break apart beneath them. Though calm to all appearances, Shackleton was becoming increasingly concerned, and began to have nightmares of crewmembers being injured or killed.

Although their time at Patience Camp was usually monotonous, there was the occasional adventure. When Thomas Orde-Lees, the crewman in charge of the motorized sledges went out to practice skiing, he was attacked by a twelve foot long sea-leopard, a vicious type of seal, which had emerged from a gap between the floes. Orde-Lees barely escaped the pursuing animal, which was shot by Wild. Worsley and Cheetham had a similarly narrow escape from a thirty foot killer whale while hunting penguins.

On March 23 the crew's spirits lifted as the men spotted land—the northern peninsula of Antarctica that juts out into the Southern Ocean. After months of drifting and waiting there was wild excitement in the camp. The crew of the *Endurance* eagerly anticipated Shackleton's command to load the sledges and begin marching, but the order never came. The Boss refused to take the risk of crossing unstable ice. Even if the floes broke apart and they took to the boats, he reasoned, there was the danger of the boats being crushed by the pack ice. He resolved to continue the drift, wait until they reached open ocean, and then sail to the closest land. The men were disappointed, but accepted Shackleton's decision because of their firmly held belief that everything he did was with their best interests in mind.

Worsley calculated that Patience Camp would likely drift beyond Paulet Island and the cache of supplies there. Once back in the boats, only two landing points would be open to them: Clarence Island and Elephant Island, and if they were unable to navigate to either, they would be carried into the sea. As April approached, the ice floe that was home to Patience Camp grew significantly smaller and weaker. On March 31, the men detected a weak swell under the ice, which meant they were close to open water. They had not experienced the ocean's swell for over a year.

Shackleton's men were rapidly nearing the end of months of living on floating ice. On April 9, the Patience Camp floe was too unstable for the men to remain on it, and they launched their three boats, the *James Caird*, the *Dudley Docker*, and the *Stancomb Wills*. The crew of the *Endurance* was finally back on the water, and they began to row for land, which was at least 60 miles away. The journey was extremely hazardous. Huge waves carried giant pieces of ice that battered the boats, while killer whales posed a constant threat. An attack by one of the creatures could easily have toppled the diminutive crafts.

After their first day of rowing, the crew made camp on an ice floe, which seemed preferable to spending the night in the boats. While the men slept in sleeping bags huddled inside their tents, Shackleton walked the ice. The floe suddenly split apart, dropping a crewman, still in his sleeping bag, into the frozen water. Shackleton hurled himself to the ice, grabbed the bag and heaved the man back on to the floe just before the gap closed.

All supplies were immediately transferred to a more stable section of the floe. During this operation, a small section of ice on which Shackleton was standing broke free, stranding him as it drifted into the darkness. Crewmembers quickly launched a boat and recovered the Boss by tracking his voice. Shackleton told Wild that "he had never felt so lonely in his life." It was agreed they would no longer leave the relative safety of the boats.

Despite the crew's hard rowing, the winds and currents had actually swept them thirty miles farther away from Elephant Island. "Shackleton did not announce this bad news to the party but simply said we had not made such good progress as expected," Wild wrote. The closest land was now Graham Land, on the Antarctic Peninsula, but as the sun rose on April 13 it became clear that thick pack ice would prevent a landing. The wind turned towards Elephant Island, which was one hundred miles away. "Worsley and I agreed with Shackleton that this was our best hope, the majority of the party being seriously exhausted," Wild recalled.

On April 14, after five days at sea, the ocean had taken an enormous toll on the crew. Large waves crashed into the tiny boats, constantly soaking the men, and the bitterly cold temperatures kept them in a permanently frozen state. "Our outer clothing was like a heavy suit of armor with no joints," Wild recalled. They went days without sleep, and their bodies ached. With no ice nearby, they no longer had a source of fresh water, and rapidly began to dehydrate. "At least half of the party were insane, fortunately not violent, simply helpless and hopeless," Wild wrote. "Again Shackleton's marvelous powers of fortitude, unselfishness and consideration for others were shown. From this time until our landing, he looked after these helpless men, just as though they were babes in arms, and all mothers will understand what I mean."

Wild, who had suffered terribly from starvation, cold and dysentery during the sledging journeys of the *Nimrod* expedition, described the night of April 14 as "the worst I have ever known." Powerful winds blew a freezing spray over the boats, and a blinding snow prevented the sailors from reading the compass or spotting Elephant Island. Wild, who sat at the tiller of the *James Caird* for the duration of the voyage, attempted to navigate by wind. "As hour after hour passed, I began to fear the wind had changed and we were sailing the wrong direction," Wild explained. "About 3 a.m. Shackleton was attending to one of the semiconscious men and asked me some question. Bearing ahead through my sore and bloodshot eyes, I had just at that moment caught a glimpse of a moonlit glacier on Elephant Island, and instead of replying to the question, I said as plainly as I was able with swollen and aching tongue and throat, 'I can see it! I can see it!' by the time Shackleton turned, the island was obscured again and he afterwards told me he had a momentary dread that 'poor old Wild's gone off his head.'"

Chapter 18 Leadership Concepts:

Keep morale high through personal communication:
While the men were stranded on the ice, Shackleton started speaking to crewmembers in small groups, endeavoring to gauge their morale and impart his optimism. Except for the period in which he suffered from a debilitating bout of sciatica, Shackleton visited each tent daily, meeting with the men personally.

Selective disbursement of information: Despite the hard rowing by the crew under terrible conditions, the winds and currents actually pushed the small boats thirty miles farther from Elephant Island. Shackleton wisely mitigated the damage this news would have had on the crew's morale, telling them only that their progress had been less than expected.

Make the practical, not the popular choice: When the crew spotted land after months of tedious drifting on the ice, they were understandably anxious to take to the boats and begin rowing. Shackleton's decision to wait until they were beyond dangerous pack ice was cautious and pragmatic. A leader more concerned with his popularity might have given in to the crew's emotions and made a rash but dangerous decision.

Chapter 19

Do or Die

As they closed on Elephant Island, the wind died down and they were forced to row, an agonizing process for men who had gone twenty-four hours without water. After ten hours of rowing they were still eight miles from their destination. During the night a strong wind came up, and all three boats took on a great deal of water. The *Caird* towed the *Wills*, but the *Docker* was soon out of sight of the other two crews.

By 8:00 a.m. on the morning of April 16 the men were able to reach ice in the water, broken off from the glaciers of Elephant Island, and satisfy their tremendous thirst. "Another 12 hours at sea would most certainly have killed at least half the party," Wild wrote. Shackleton took the *Wills* nearer to the coast (he did not want to risk damaging the *Caird*, the largest of the three boats), to search out a suitable landing place. The *Docker* reappeared, much to the relief of the crews of the *Caird* and *Wills*.

By the time they landed at Elephant Island, Shackleton had not slept in eight days, while Worsley had slept only a few hours, and Wild just a few minutes. Worsley told the Boss that his efforts had been nothing short of superhuman, to which Shackleton replied "Superhuman effort…isn't worth a damn unless it achieves results."

Months of life on only ice and water had proved too much for some of the men. Shackleton and Wild watched as many of the crew laughed hysterically while rolling around on the rocky beach. Some men buried their faces in the stones or poured handfuls over their heads. Other shoved the small rocks in their pockets.

After they were given a hot drink and a meal of cooked seal meat, the men of the *Endurance* were able to gather themselves and assess their situation. Elephant Island provided solid ground to stand on, access to ice they could melt for drinking water, and seals, elephant seals, and penguins to hunt for food. However, it soon became clear that the island was far from paradise. The gravelly beach and mountainous interior provided little cover from the vicious, freezing winds, and no one knew how long the food supply would last. When the penguins, seals and sea-elephants all disappeared one day, the men were most alarmed. Luckily a flock of penguins soon emerged and over one hundred were quickly killed.

Many members of the crew were already suffering from the effects of the bitter cold. Eight of them were physically unable to work, while others were extremely depressed. As always, Shackleton remained cheerful and active, constantly trying to maintain morale.

April 18 was Frank Wild's forty-third birthday. "Though I have spent many tough ones in my life, this was without doubt the worst ever," he reminisced. "Almost the whole day was spent under our flattened tents, in soaking clothing and sleeping bags." Shackleton and Charles Green, the cook, built a makeshift shelter for the stove, brewed a teeming stew, and delivered it to each tent. "This was entirely unexpected, but all the more appreciated," Wild wrote.

Shackleton, Worsley and Wild met in private to discuss their next steps. Rescue was extremely unlikely. No one in the world had reason to think the crew of the *Endurance* would be marooned on Elephant Island, and there was little chance of any ships stopping there or even passing close by, as the island was encompassed by reefs, rocks, pack ice and icebergs. In fact, Shackleton and his crew were probably the first humans to ever set foot on the remote isle.

The three men considered their options. It would be certain disaster to have the entire crew return to the boats and sail for another island. Physically, many of the men were in no condition to battle the elements on the open ocean. The boats, too, were battered, and had suffered serious damage, including broken oars, during the landing. Shackleton told Worsley that a boat journey would have to be made, despite the enormous risk of sailing a small boat through the Southern Ocean. He was determined not to let the crew starve to death.

Worsley recognized the importance of Shackleton's presence to the men and volunteered to command the boat journey. Shackleton answered him simply: "No, that's my job." Worsley reminded Shackleton of his skill in sailing, navigation, and surf landings in an attempt to dissuade him. Shackleton smiled and replied "Don't worry, Skipper, you'll be with me, anyway." Wild volunteered for the mission, but Shackleton needed him to remain on Elephant Island as commander. Wild asked Shackleton if Crean could stay behind with him, but Crean "begged so hard to go that I said no more about it," Wild recalled.

The situation had forced Shackleton into a decision he was uncomfortable with. He did not want to leave his men, or even tell them he was going to leave. He was also concerned that if the end result was bad, he might be accused of abandoning them. He addressed the crew, explained the realities of their chances for rescue and survival, then told them he was going to take a boat and sail for help. If the plan was successful, rescue could be anticipated in four to five weeks. He told them plainly, "I'm afraid it's a forlorn hope, and I don't ask anyone to come who has not thoroughly weighed the chances." Despite the suffering of the prior months, the extreme hardships the crew of the boat journey would certainly endure, and the enormous risk, every man instantly volunteered.

Veteran sailors John Vincent and Tim McCarthy were chosen for the voyage, as was Chippy McNeish, the carpenter who had rebelled against the exhausting relaying of the boats across the ice. Port Stanley in the Falkland Islands was five hundred forty miles away, but lay in the opposite direction of the prevailing winds and currents. Shackleton and Worsley agreed their target would have to be South Georgia Island, home of the Stromness whaling station the *Endurance* had left from sixteen months earlier, and which lay eight hundred miles away.

The *James Caird*, the largest of the three small boats at just over twenty-two feet, was selected for the journey. McNeish used the mast from the *Stancomb Wills* to strengthen the keel of the *James Caird*, and while there was not enough wood to create a true deck, a frame for one was created using sledge runners and box lids. A frozen length of canvas was thawed out one foot at a time over a blubber stove, then stretched over part of the boat and nailed into place, providing the only covering that would protect the sailors from the constant onslaught of freezing waves. "It certainly gave an appearance of safety to the boat, though I had an uneasy feeling that it bore a strong likeness to stage scenery," Shackleton wrote. Marston, the expedition artist, used his oil paints mixed with seal's blood to caulk the seams, making the *James Caird* as seaworthy as possible.

Worsley and Shackleton disagreed about the amount of ballast the small boat would require. Shackleton was gravely concerned that the *James Caird* would capsize in rough seas, and insisted on over a ton of ballast. Worsley believed that half of that would be sufficient, as the weight of the men and stores would add additional weight. Shackleton prevailed in this debate.

Food rations for thirty days were stored, along with drinking water, fuel, matches, a portable stove, six sleeping bags, a rifle, and navigational instruments and charts. The expedition doctors, Macklin and McIlroy, urged Shackleton to take Blackborrow. The young stowaway was suffering from frostbitten toes, and the physicians feared gangrene would set in if he remained on Elephant Island where they had limited ability to treat him. Shackleton, though very concerned over Blackborrow's health, realized that adding an ill man to the crew would jeopardize all of them. Blackborrow stayed behind.

On April 24 the *James Caird* left Elephant Island. Immediately upon launch, a wave toppled the boat and McNeish and Vincent were thrown overboard. Two men traded clothes with McNeish and Vincent so they could at least begin their journey with dry clothes. The generous donors would suffer in wet clothes for two weeks. Shackleton was concerned with the mental toll the event would have on the men on Elephant Island. "I'm sorry they saw that stroke of bad luck," he told Worsley, "I hope they don't take it as an omen."

"We gave them three hearty cheers and watched the boat getting smaller and smaller in the distance; then, seeing some of the party in tears, I immediately sent them all to work," Wild wrote. "My own heart was very full. I heard one of the few pessimists remark, 'That's the last of them,' and almost knocked him down with a rock, but satisfied myself by addressing a few remarks to him in real lower deck language."

Worsley steered the *James Caird* north in an effort to escape pack ice that was rapidly forming around the island. By nightfall they were free of the ice, and Shackleton sent everyone except Worsley below to rest. Shackleton told his Captain "We've had some great adventures together, Skipper, but this is the greatest adventure of all. This time it really is do or die, as they say in the story-books." Shackleton retained a boyish quality that amused Worsley. He enjoyed receiving praise, and displayed an interest in finding hidden treasure. Shackleton spoke of possibly finding gold in Antarctica, noting that he had found coal at the Beardmore Glacier. He was also keenly interested in a pearl lagoon Worsley had seen in the Pacific.

Shackleton confided in Worsley that he was "dead against" separating the crew, but that clearly there was no choice. One of Wild's challenges, Shackleton noted, would be to find activities to keep the men occupied as the unique blend of boredom and suspense would make them difficult to deal with. According to Wordie, the entire crew had great confidence in Wild, and his stature as a leader only increased during their time on Elephant Island.

Shackleton established a strict routine of hot meals and drinks every four hours for the small crew of the *James Caird*. He kept a watchful eye on each man, and if one seemed particularly cold or was shivering, Shackleton would have a hot drink (scalding water with milk power) served immediately.

The Boss would not disclose who the drink was for, so that no one man would become unduly anxious about himself.

Conditions on the boat could not have been worse. The men were soaked by constant waves that crashed over them. What little sleep they were able to get below the canvas covering was cramped and uncomfortable. The men often awoke in their sleeping bags with a feeling of being smothered and buried alive.

While three men slept, the other three worked, with one steering and two pumping water from the boat. This job was particularly difficult, as one man had to hold a brass tube against the bottom of the boat with his bare hands while another pushed the handle up and down. The men pumping took turns every five minutes, and each hour the men would rotate jobs until the next watch relieved them.

When the *James Caird* had traveled approximately 150 miles from Elephant Island, the men had an excellent run and covered 83 miles in one day. Their spirits were lifted, and they grew more optimistic. Shackleton asked Worsley if he thought they would make it, and Worsley replied that with luck they might reach South Georgia in eight days. Shackleton agreed, stating "A lot depends on luck."

Shackleton was concerned that the cooking fuel might not last the entire journey. "What our life would be on this boat without hot drinks I dare not imagine," he told Worsley. A second fear was that the wind might force them back into the pack ice. The next morning, when a very cold wind reached them from the south, the men realized that the ice was closer than they had hoped. That night, the waves became too strong to sail through in the dark, and the decision was made to drop the sea anchor. They were temporarily safer, but were losing precious traveling time. The powerful waves and lower temperatures created a layer of ice on the thin canvas that stretched over part of the boat. The ice kept the waves out, providing a temporary respite from the constant drenching.

To Shackleton, the night at anchor provided an opportunity for the men to get some badly needed rest. At nine p.m., he announced "No watch tonight, boys. There's nothing to watch—no bergs, no ships and nothing to trouble us. So we'll all go to sleep while we are hove-to; nothing can happen to us."

By ten the men were asleep, but at three a.m. the men awoke, struck by an uneasy feeling they could not immediately identify. It soon became apparent that a thick sheet of ice had encased the hull and was sinking the *James Caird*. The men quickly chopped handholds and footholds in the ice, and one man was sent up the mass of ice to begin the brutal process of chipping it away. This task was so difficult, working in the bitter cold, in the dark, clinging to the ice as the ship bucked in the waves, that Shackleton rotated men every four minutes. The climb back into the boat was equally perilous. Vincent slipped, slid across the ice covered canvas, and was just able to grab the mast before falling overboard. It took two hours of grueling labor to free the ship.

It is difficult to imagine the dangers and discomforts endured by the crew of the *James Caird*. The sleeping bags, made of reindeer skin on the outside and hair on the inside, began to molt from the constant wetness. Hair was everywhere on the boat, in the men's eyes, noses, and mouths as they tried to sleep, in the vital water pump, and even in their food. In spite of these difficulties, the crew performed brilliantly and without complaint. McCarthy stood out for his remarkable cheerfulness even in the most dismal conditions. When Worsley would relieve him, McCarthy would state with a smile "It's a grand day, sir."

Chapter 19 Leadership Concepts:

The Power of Responsibility: The lives of each of the men meant more to Shackleton than anything else, and his men knew it. His commitment to them, made evident in his words and deeds, engendered tremendous trust and loyalty in the crew.

The Power of Psychology: Shackleton was careful to help a man in trouble without singling him out—ordering hot drinks for everyone when one man was getting too cold, thus keeping up the confidence of each individual and maintaining the group's morale.

Chapter 20

October Would Be Too Late

Eight days after leaving Elephant Island, the *James Caird* was over halfway to South Georgia. The crew spoke of a belief that many sailors share—that what they have already done, they can do again. Passing the halfway mark was therefore cause for hopefulness, but the journey was far from over.

While Shackleton was steering during the night he observed a long white line in the distance, so long and high that he mistook it for a clearing sky. Moments later, he realized the white line was actually the crest of a tidal wave. He yelled to the men "Hang on for your lives!" as the giant wave crashed over the boat. "During twenty-six years' experience of the ocean in all its moods I had never seen a wave so gigantic," Shackleton remembered. "We felt our boat lifted and flung forward like a cork in breaking surf. We were in a seething chaos of tortured water; but somehow the boat lived through it…we bailed with the energy of men fighting for life."

On the night of their tenth day at sea, Worsley found himself locked in the sitting position after completing his turn at the helm. The other men dragged him below the decking and massaged his legs until he could straighten them and slide into his sleeping bag.

By Day 13, the *James Caird* was finally closing on South Georgia. Worsley's navigation had to be precise, because if they missed South Georgia they would be unable to turn into the wind and currents, and would almost certainly die before they could reach the coast of Africa. On the fourteenth day, they observed kelp in the water, then birds, both signs of nearby land. At one p.m. in the afternoon, they spotted the mountainous peaks of South Georgia. The light faded quickly on the winter day, and Worsley suggested they attempt a landing in the dark. He sensed foul weather and was concerned about remaining out at sea. To make matters worse, the men were down to their last keg of fresh water, which had been contaminated with sea water when it fell into the surf while being loaded onto the *James Caird* on Elephant Island. It was potable, but drinking it only made them thirstier. The dreaded reindeer hairs were in the water as well.

"Thirst took possession of us," Shackleton wrote, but he could not risk increasing the already small daily ration of water. If the boat were to be blown away from the island, the voyage might have to be extended for days. "Lack of water is always the most severe privation which men can be condemned to endure," he wrote. "I had to be very firm in refusing to allow anyone to anticipate the morrow's allowance, which I was sometimes begged to do."

Shackleton was eager to end the suffering of the crew, but also hesitant to attempt the landing, owing to the darkness and the presence of "blind rollers," powerful waves breaking over the outlying reefs of South Georgia. He decided to wait until morning, so they sailed back out to sea, out of sight of the land. Despite his reputation as a fearless adventurer, Shackleton, according to Worsley, was very cautious, and undertook risks only when absolutely necessary.

The next morning, their fifteenth since leaving Elephant Island, the *James Caird* was hit by an extremely powerful storm as it approached South Georgia. The harsh weather prevented them from seeing the land, but they knew it must be close. They feared being hurled against the rocks, and were suddenly more eager to avoid South Georgia than they had been to find it.

They fought the storm for over ten hours, and the harder they worked, the greater their thirst became. It appeared the ship was doomed to wreck on the rocks, and Worsley thought to himself what a pity it was that they had accomplished such a tremendous journey but that no one would ever know. A lucky shift in wind and current suddenly guided the *James Caird* to safety, and they sailed for the natural harbor of King Haakon Sound.

The next morning the crew still had not obtained water or ice. Their mouths and throats were so dry that they were unable to eat, and searched anxiously for any ice they could find floating in the Sound. It was indeed ironic that men who had spent so many months living on vast floes were now desperate to find even the smallest piece of ice.

By nightfall they had landed in a small cove. As three men held the boat from drifting back into the water, Shackleton climbed some rocks with a rope to secure it. "A slip on the wet rocks twenty feet up nearly closed my part of the story just as we were achieving safety," he wrote. Shackleton was caught by a jagged edge of rock that saved his life but left him badly bruised. That night, Shackleton admitted to Worsley he had been wrong about the amount of ballast needed on the *James Caird*, and that the journey would have been shorter if the boat had carried less weight. Worsley was impressed—other leaders he had known would not have been as willing to own up to a mistake.

As the men hauled the boat up the shore, they happily realized they were standing in a stream of fresh water. "We heard a gurgling sound which was sweet music in our ears," Shackleton recalled, "It was a splendid moment." As they drank from the stream, the men reflected on their arduous journey. They could barely move their arms and legs due to the constant wetness and the cramped conditions on the *James Caird*. They had been so confined that they had not been able to sit upright while eating, and their digestion had suffered greatly.

The men found a cave in a nearby cliff, and five slept while one kept watch over the boat. At two in the morning, they awoke to the shouts of Crean, who was desperately trying to hold onto the boat while it was being carried out to sea. The boulder to which the craft had been secured had been pulled from the ground by the force of the water. The men retrieved Crean and the boat, then held onto it for the remainder of the night, out of fear it would be lost. The crew was exhausted, their spirits low, but they enjoyed a laugh when Shackleton, in a very formal tone joked "I do hope that you are all enjoying my little party." The next day they feasted on albatross stew and got some badly needed rest.

The landing on South Georgia was only the beginning of yet another dangerous adventure. The *James Caird* had come ashore on the opposite side of the island from the whaling station, and the danger of being crushed against the reef or swept out to sea made it too risky to attempt a voyage around the island. Worse yet, the boat had lost its rudder during the landing, making steering impossible. Shackleton had only one choice—to walk across South Georgia—which would require scaling the uncharted mountains and glaciers that stood between his team and the Stromness whaling port.

The crew took a few days to rest and recover from the boat journey. They were relatively comfortable, as they had seals, sea elephants, penguins and albatross for food, and access to fresh water. Shackleton and Worsley walked from the cove in King Haakon Sound into the interior of South Georgia, searching for a starting point for their journey. Giant glaciers barred their path, and they decided it would be necessary to sail to the head of King Haakon Sound, and begin the trek inland from there. Without a rudder, however, the trip would be difficult, if not impossible. An oar was rigged to act as a rudder, but Worsley doubted it would work.

Shackleton selected Worsley and Crean to join him on the overland journey as McNeish, Vincent and McCarthy were still weak from the boat trip. Just as the *James Caird* was being launched Worsley spotted something in the surf. Crean went out to retrieve it, and came back with the rudder. The unexpected find was so providential that the men believed they were under the watchful eye of some protective force.

Shackleton grew impatient as the weather prevented them from beginning the inland journey, but as conditions improved so did his mood. At two a.m. on May 19, they began their crossing under a bright moon. The mountain climbing was slow work but they managed to ascend the rocky slopes. McNeish, the carpenter, had set eight two inch brass screws into the soles of each of their boots to help with traction.

When mist and fog formed, almost completely obscuring their vision, the trio found themselves teetering at the edge of dark, deep pit, having narrowly escaped falling in. They could not understand how such a large pit had formed, but theorized that a meteorite might have been the cause. From this point forward they roped together for safety.

As they climbed higher up the mountain the temperature dropped. Shackleton's feet were freezing, partly because he was wearing leather boots, rather than the standard gear used on the expedition. There had been a shortage of boots, and Shackleton had given his pair to another man. The Boss had a personal rule that he should suffer any deprivation before any member of the crew.

The mountains of South Georgia formed five peaks, and the men hoped to descend one of the four passes between them to reach the opposite side of the island. They discovered the first three passes led to steep, sheer drops, but when the fourth pass proved equally impossible to navigate, Shackleton, Worsley and Crean found themselves with their backs to the wall. As night began to fall, they knew they had to get down, or they would certainly die of exposure. With fog behind and darkness below, they could go neither back or forward.

They first attempted to descend the slope by cutting steps into the ice, but after covering only one hundred yards in thirty minutes, it became clear this method would not work. Shackleton suggested the men sit in a row on top of their coiled rope and slide down the mountain. "It's a devil of a risk, but we've got to take it," Shackleton stated. They slid, very fast, down the steep slope of the mountain, and were surprised to find themselves grinning and yelling with excitement. After about a mile they began to slow down as the slope leveled off, and landed in soft snow. Unhurt and relieved, they shook hands. "It's not good to do that kind of thing too often," Shackleton joked.

At seven a.m. on May 20, 1916, the steam whistle blew at the Stromness whaling station. It was the first sound of civilization Shackleton, Worsley and Crean had heard in almost two years. They rappelled down a final obstacle, an icy waterfall, and by mid-afternoon they arrived at the whaling station. They had been marching up and down mountains, with no sleep and stopping only for meals, for thirty-six hours.

The three men on the other side of South Georgia were quickly rescued by Worsley and two Norwegian sailors. McNeish, Vincent and McCarthy expressed surprise that at least one of the men of the *James Caird* was not part of the rescue party. Although they had been with Worsley every day for two years, they did not recognize him after he had shaved, bathed, and changed clothes. "Our first night at the whaling station was blissful," Shackleton recalled, as he and Crean shared a bedroom that was "so comfortable we could not sleep." A heavy snowstorm, which began just after their arrival at Stromness, continued into the next day, and might have meant the end for Shackleton, Wild and Crean had it started any earlier and trapped them in the mountains.

The sailors and captains of the British and Norwegian whaling ships were quick to offer their assistance in rescuing the crew stranded on Elephant Island. The British whaler *Southern Sky*, steam driven and made of steel, was available, but as there was no telegraph on South Georgia, Shackleton could not contact the owners. He told the local British magistrate that he would take personal responsibility for the ship, and "wrote out an agreement with Lloyd's for the insurance of the ship." Norwegian Captain Ingvar Thoms, who had befriended Shackleton at Stromness in 1914 volunteered to serve as Captain. On the eve of the rescue mission, Shackleton regaled veteran whaling captains with the story of the *James Caird*. "It was pleasant to tell the men who knew these sullen treacherous southern seas, and they congratulated us on having accomplished a remarkable boat journey."

The *Southern Sky* steamed towards Elephant Island, but soon encountered the pounding of heavy pack ice that Shackleton knew the steel hull could not endure. After six days at sea, the ship was five hundred miles from the Falkland

Islands and six hundred from South Georgia. Shackleton decided to head towards the Falklands and obtain another ship. On May 31 he reached Port Stanley on the Falklands, and finally had access to the outside world via telegraph. He cabled the King to provide an update on the status of the expedition, and received a reply the following day: "Rejoice to hear of your safe arrival in the Falkland Islands and trust your comrades on Elephant Island may soon be rescued."

Shackleton sought out a rescue ship, ideally one made of wood. The British Admiralty told him that no such ship was currently accessible, but one could probably be sent to him by October. "I replied that October would be too late," Shackleton recalled. "I was bent upon the rescue of my comrades at the earliest possible moment, for I was fully conscious that the lives of some of them might be the price of unnecessary delay."

Uruguay sent what Shackleton described as a "stout little vessel," the *Instituo de Pesca No. 1* to Port Stanley on June 10, and a second relief mission was quickly underway. The ship was less than twenty miles from Elephant Island when pack ice stopped it cold. With only three days of coal left, Shackleton ordered the ship back to Port Stanley. Uruguay offered another ship, but it would have to be dry docked and repaired before sailing, and Shackleton could not afford to wait. Shackleton, Worsley and Crean travelled to Punta Arenas and obtained the *Emma*, which was towed towards Elephant Island by the Chilean steamer *Yelcho*. On July 14th, during a powerful gale, the tow rope between the two ships snapped. "With the crack of a gun it broke," Shackleton recalled.

On July 21st the *Emma* was within one hundred miles of Elephant Island. The *Emma* was "tossing like a cork in the swell, and after a few bumps I saw that she was actually lighter than the fragments of ice around her," Shackleton wrote. As this third attempt failed, Shackleton grew increasingly desperate, knowing his men might be facing starvation.

On August 8 they arrived in Port Stanley, and learned that the British Admiralty had arranged for Scott's ship, the *Discovery*, to be sent to the Falkland Islands by mid-September. The Governor of the Falklands suggested Shackleton wait for the arrival of the *Discovery*, but "I could not be content to wait six or seven weeks, knowing that 600 miles away my comrades were in desperate need." Shackleton wrote. He begged the Chilean government to loan him the use of the *Yelcho*, even though it was, like the *Southern Sky*, made of steel and not suited for contact with heavy pack ice. Chile agreed, and on August 25 Shackleton started south on a fourth rescue attempt.

"This time Providence favoured us," Shackleton recalled. As the *Yelcho* approached Elephant Island, Shackleton found the ice had been pushed north by a gale, and he had his opportunity. On the morning of August 30 they approached the island, and a lifting fog exposed the camp.

For the men on Elephant Island, the situation had been almost unbearable. They had dealt with bitter cold, boredom, and the growing fear of never being rescued. The men had attempted to construct a cave, but found it impossible. Four foot high stone walls were built, and the two boats were placed on the walls upside down. Tent canvas was extended from the edge of the boats to the ground, with snow packed around the canvas to trap what little heat was created by the stove. Inside the makeshift shelter it was cramped, dark, and impossible to stand up. Wild carefully managed the sleeping arrangements, and he dealt with arguments over inches of space. "I had to go along and tell one or other to move over, and could not turn in myself until all the naughty children were nicely tucked up," he wrote.

Wild created small windows by slicing the canvas and using small pieces of glass from instruments salvaged from the *Endurance*. This let in some light and greatly improved the spirits of the men. Wild also arranged for Hussey to give weekly banjo performances, which helped keep up morale. A rotation system was used so that all the men would have an equal opportunity to eat near the heat of the stove. When some food was stolen, Wild threatened strong repercussions if it were to happen again. It didn't. Wordie recorded in his diary that Wild was quickly establishing himself as a quality leader.

Blackborrow's frostbitten toes became gangrenous, as Drs. McIlroy and Macklin had feared. Under the overturned boats, using candlelight, the two physicians amputated the toes, preventing the spread of gangrene and saving the young stowaway's life.

By late August it had been close to four months since Shackleton and the crew of the *James Caird* had left Elephant Island. After expecting rescue in four or five weeks, the men were losing hope, in spite of Wild's best efforts. As the seals and penguins migrated away, the food supply had become dangerously low and the men grew increasingly concerned about the very real possibility of starvation. On the morning of August 30, 1916, Wild gave his daily shout: "Lash up and stow, boys, the Boss may come today!" Unlike earlier exhortations, that day the words proved true. Shackleton rowed from the *Yelcho* to the rocky shores of Elephant Island, trying to count the number of figures on the beach. When close enough, he shouted "Are you all well?" and Wild replied that they were.

The crew of the *Endurance* received enthusiastic receptions in Punta Arenas and Valparaiso, where thirty thousand people turned out to welcome them. Shackleton travelled by train across the Andes to personally thank the President of Chile. Shackleton and Worsley then continued on to Panama and San Francisco, where they boarded a steamer for New Zealand. Shackleton had one more rescue mission to complete.

Chapter 20 Leadership Concepts:

Be Cautious, But Take Risks When Necessary: Shackleton was proud of his reputation among the men for carefulness, but he would take calculated chances when forced to, including the makeshift toboggan ride down the mountain.

Deal With Serious Issues Quickly: When food was stolen on Elephant Island, Wild made it clear that any recurrence would be dealt with severely. His prompt response ended what could have become a cause of major dissension among the crew. Wild also settled petty differences and kept the men on Elephant Island as positive as possible considering the gravity of their situation.

Keep Your Sense of Humor: Even in the most trying of circumstances, Shackleton would joke with his men, which helped keep their spirits up.

Admit Your Mistakes: Shackleton acknowledged to Worsley that he had been wrong about the ballast—which impressed the Captain about Shackleton's character.

Sacrifice: The Boss had a personal rule that he should suffer any deprivation before any member of the crew. This approach added to the trust and loyalty the crew felt for him.

Chapter 21

Almost Human

The epic tale of the *Endurance* was only half the story of Shackleton's Imperial Trans-Antarctic Expedition. It was left to the men of the *Aurora* to land on the opposite side of the continent and lay the vital depots that would keep Shackleton and his team alive as they completed the second leg of their journey.

The Ross Sea Party, charged by Shackleton with this crucial task, was led by Aenaes Mackintosh, who had lost an eye in the accident aboard the *Nimrod* in 1908. After returning to England following that expedition, Mackintosh had married Gladys Campbell, and was working at Liverpool's Imperial Merchant Service Guild when Shackleton asked him to serve as Captain of the *Aurora*. It would be Mackintosh's job to sail the ship into the Ross Sea, secure a landing point, and create a base of operations. From there dog teams would deliver the crucial caches of food and fuel to designated points on the Barrier. Mackintosh, deeply loyal to Shackleton, resigned from the Guild, and left Gladys with their two infant daughters.

A key member of the *Aurora* team was Ernest Joyce, veteran of both the *Discovery* and *Nimrod* expeditions and an experienced sledger. Shackleton chose Joyce to be "in charge of all equipment, stores, sledges, clothing, dogs, etc.," for the Ross

Sea Party and to oversee the depot laying. Support crew included Frank Wild's younger brother Ernest, and cousins Irvine Gaze and Arnold Spencer-Smith. At 31, Spencer-Smith was a graduate of Cambridge and an ordained Episcopalian reverend. He would serve as the *Aurora's* photographer and chaplain.

Dick Richards had answered an ad in a Melbourne newspaper seeking a physicist keen on an exciting journey to the Southern Continent. At only twenty-one and having just completed his undergraduate degree in physics, Richards thought he might be considered too green, and was somewhat astonished when a telegram arrived requesting an interview. After a six-hundred mile train trip to Sydney, Richards found himself aboard the *Aurora* being interviewed by Mackintosh. The Captain explained the nature of the job, which would include taking scientific recordings of local weather, animal life, and the general surroundings. Since Shackleton preferred that veterans be responsible for the crucial work of depot laying, Mackintosh told Richards it was unlikely he would do much sledging.

The *Aurora* steamed out of Sydney Harbor on December 15, 1914, and arrived in Hobart, Tasmania, a week later. On the 23rd, Tasmanian Governor Sir William Macartney toured the ship with his wife, Lady Ettie Macartney, who was none other than Robert Scott's sister. Lady Macartney gave Joyce, who had served under Scott on board *Discovery*, a portrait of her beloved brother.

December 24th was spent loading stores and dogs on board, and on Christmas Day the *Aurora* sailed for Antarctica. The ship anchored in McMurdo Sound in the Ross Sea at Cape Evans, near the hut built by Scott's men in 1910 during the *Terra Nova* expedition. The ship could have docked further south, at Hut Point (the location of the Discovery Hut, built during Scott's 1902 journey), but Shackleton had warned Mackintosh not to anchor the *Aurora* too far south, fearing it would become locked in ice.

With no means of communication between the two ships, Mackintosh and Joyce had no way of knowing the *Endurance* was already trapped, and that Shackleton would either be delayed in reaching Antarctica or never get there at all. Shackleton had given Joyce written instructions prior to their departure: "Well, Joyce, old chap...if there is one man I can trust to lay the depots it is your good self—that was proved at a critical time in 1908 when I returned from the long trek south...Take charge of all sledging equipment and...lay the food-fuel depots along the same course as in previous expeditions."

Mackintosh had orders from Shackleton as well. "Make a base at some convenient spot in McMurdo Sound, land stores and equipment, and lay depots on the Great Ice Barrier down to the Beardmore Glacier to support the party coming across the continent from the Weddell Sea coast." Both Mackintosh and Joyce felt a strong personal devotion to Shackleton, and the enormous responsibility of laying the depots for a polar team that would surely perish if they descended the Beardmore Glacier and found no stores of food and fuel. But Mackintosh and Joyce also had different views about when and how to lay the depots, and Shackleton's failure to clearly delineate authority over this aspect of the expedition would have grave consequences in the cold months to come.

The plan called for supply depots to be laid in stages at points progressively further south. The caches would be placed at every latitudinal degree, about sixty miles apart, along the Great Ice Barrier to the foot of the Beardmore Glacier. When Shackleton and his men descended the Beardmore, life-saving food and fuel would be waiting for them, and they could then depot hop on the return journey to Hut Point and safety. "The importance of the task was enormous," Joyce recalled years later, "for on its fulfillment rested the lives of the Shackleton party."

Sledging would take place in stages, first to Hut Point, then to Minna Bluff, the large and easily recognizable outcropping of rock on the Barrier. From there, further depots would be laid, including a sizeable one at 80 degrees south, which would be used as a base for the most southern depots, including the final one near the Beardmore Glacier. Mackintosh was anxious to lay the 80 degree depot as soon as possible, and by January 1915 the sledging to Hut Point had begun.

The depot laying was highly strenuous work, as it required the men and dogs to drag food and fuel for themselves and for Shackleton's men. Joyce was concerned that the dogs, not yet in pulling condition after their confinement on the ship, should not be overworked on the initial sledging journey, and voiced his concerns to Mackintosh. In February a sledging journey to the Bluff was made. One dog died, and Joyce, with far more sledging experience than Mackintosh, warned his Captain that they would be wise to rest the canines now, saving them for the much longer treks that lay ahead.

Mackintosh compromised, and agreed to send the weakest dogs back north with three men while he, Joyce and Wild proceeded south with the nine stronger dogs. The push to 80 degrees began, and after brutal pulling through blizzard conditions, the men arrived at their destination on February 20. As they built the depot, a blizzard descended upon them. The men and dogs suffered terribly, and by March 2 eight of the nine dogs had perished. "There is only one survivor: Pinkey," Joyce wrote. On the return journey north, Joyce noted that Wild, whose feet were frostbitten, and Pinkey were "having a busman's holiday...riding on the sledge," but Pinkey died soon after. "We are sad," Joyce recorded, "On polar journeys the dogs seem almost human. One never feels lonely when they are around."

On March 10 Wild, Mackintosh and Joyce reached the Bluff, but the rare gift of a clear sky brought only bad news. They had laid the initial Bluff Depot four miles east of where it should have been, and where Shackleton would look for it. The three men, having gone nine hours since their last hot meal or rest, packed a sledge with supplies and hauled it to the correct spot.

Frostbitten and exhausted, the trio withstood yet another blizzard, built the new depot, then marched fifty miles in temperatures that plummeted to minus 70 degrees. Finally they reached Safety Camp, at the edge of the Barrier, and food. "After being on the Barrier for sixty days we managed to crawl back to Hut Point. It was a good thing the doctor was there, for Wild had to have one toe and one ear amputated," Joyce wrote. The crucial depot at 80 degrees had been laid before the onset of winter as Mackintosh had wished, but it was a Pyrrhic victory. Mackintosh, Joyce and the rest of the Ross Sea Party now faced the prospect of much longer depot laying journeys still ahead of them, with their nine strongest dogs already dead.

On March 11, Joseph Stenhouse, in command of *Aurora* in Mackintosh's absence, picked up six men at Hut Point and returned to Cape Evans. Mackintosh, Joyce and Wild had not yet returned, but Stenhouse was eager to get the ship north of Hut Point, fearing it might become locked in the ice. On March 14, Stenhouse gave orders to anchor the ship just off Cape Evans, where it could serve as a base of operations. While some of the scientists settled into the nearby Discovery Hut, other crewman stayed on board the ship and only a limited amount of supplies were unloaded as the men could easily walk from the ship to the hut. The *Aurora* was anchored into solid rock, which was preferable to ice which could calve and break off into the sea at any moment.

The Ross Sea Party was now operating as three units: Stenhouse and the men who lived on the *Aurora* docked at Cape Evans, the scientific party who lived in the Discovery Hut near the ship, and a group including Mackintosh and Joyce who were living further south in the Terra Nova Hut at Hut Point. Once the sea ice hardened Mackintosh and his men planned to walk the thirteen miles that separated them from the *Aurora* and their comrades. They estimated the ice would be firm enough for this crossing by early June.

On the night of May 6, the young physicist Dick Richards walked out of the Discovery Hut at three in the morning to take instrument readings. He glanced routinely at the ship, but to Richards' shock and horror, the *Aurora* was gone.

Chapter 21 Leadership Concept:

Be Clear When Delegating Authority: Shackleton's orders to Joyce and Mackintosh were both vague and overlapping. This led to disagreements, compromises, and poor decisions that could have been avoided with more definitive charges.

Chapter 22

A Note for Captain Scott

The *Aurora* had been ripped from its moorings at Cape Evans by a violent gale and blown out to sea. When a particularly vicious blizzard hit and lingered for three days, the scientific party at Cape Evans feared the ship might well have been lost with all hands.

The *Aurora*, though, had survived. Stenhouse and the crew were alive, but within a few days it became clear to them that heavy ice would make impossible to make an immediate return to Cape Evans. Soon the ship became locked in ice and began drifting northward. The best that could be hoped for now was to wait for a thaw and try to reach the men in September.

On June 1 the sea ice between the Discovery Hut at Cape Evans and the Terra Nova Hut was thick enough to allow safe passage across. Mackintosh, Joyce and four others crossed the ice and arrived at the Discovery Hut, greeted by the barking of the five surviving dogs. Mackintosh and Joyce now learned of the disappearance of the *Aurora*, and the gravity of their situation. No clothing, food, or sledging gear had been put ashore before the *Aurora* had disappeared, and although Scott's hut held a good deal of basic provisions, there was no fuel. For fresh meat and fuel, the men would have to slaughter seals to survive. Besides having to keep themselves alive under very difficult conditions, the men were still committed to laying the depots for Shackleton's team. An inventory of stores was taken, and they prepared for the arduous task ahead.

The *Aurora,* meanwhile, remained trapped, and Stenhouse made plans to abandon the ship if it began implode under the intense pressure of the pack ice. The crew worked anxiously to repair the ship's damaged rudder, for even if the ship survived until a thaw it would be impossible to steer without a functioning rudder.

At Cape Evans, the men killed seals, rummaged for abandoned provisions, and pondered their situation. Mackintosh gave them an honest appraisal. If the *Aurora* was lost they could be trapped for two years, if not more, waiting for a relief ship. They would need to kill about five hundred seals a year, and be inventive and economical with the resources they had. Wild and Joyce, for example, worked tirelessly to cut a large canvas tent into extra sets of clothes for each man. Despite their situation, Mackintosh kept the men optimistic, "cheerful and bright," Joyce wrote. Mackintosh decided a trek to Shackleton's Nimrod Hut at Cape Royds might prove useful, and sledged there with geologist Alexander Stevens. The trip was worthwhile: they discovered food, tobacco, and a few precious bars of soap.

On August 12, disaster was averted when a fire in the Discovery Hut was quickly extinguished. Ten days later light returned to Antarctica, and Reverend Spencer-Smith officiated at a ceremony marking the event. Mackintosh now focused on his sledging plans, as there were many more depots to be laid. Teams soon began sledging two tons of stores onto the Barrier.

On September 17, Stenhouse marked one year since the *Aurora* had left London. Since being dislodged from its moorings and wedged in ice, the ship had drifted almost seven hundred miles.

Soon the men of the Ross Sea Party began the second phase of their depot laying. In early October nine men trekked to Hut Point, and from there started a series of trips to the Minna Bluff Depot. Their first arrangement, with all nine men dragging three sledges behind them resulted in very little progress. Joyce argued with Mackintosh about the futility of this type of sledging, and the Captain agreed to a new arrangement. He would go forward with Spencer-Smith and

Wild, pulling one sledge with a reduced weight, enabling them to travel much faster. Joyce would be in command of two other teams of three men and one sledge each who would follow at their best pace. Joyce's group consisted of Richards, Jack, Gaze, Hayward, Cope and four dogs. Joyce also lowered the weight on his sledges, which improved the morale of his men.

By October 19, Mackintosh had reached Bluff Depot, and Joyce arrived two days later. The following day, Joyce's team turned north, and on October 26, during his return journey from the Bluff to Hut Point, Joyce discovered an upturned sledge. Attached to the sledge was a note from Apsley Cherry-Garrard left for Captain Scott. "Dear Sir, We leave this morning with the dogs for Hut Point. We have made no depots, being off course all the way, and so have not been able to leave you a note before. Yours sincerely, Apsley Cherry-Garrard." (The note was discovered in 1960 under Joyce's pillow in the Cape Evans Hut).

For the Ross Sea Party, depot laying continued, more or less as planned. The depot parties had been traveling as two teams, one under the command of Mackintosh, the other under Joyce. When one of Joyce's Primus stoves began to malfunction, it became necessary to reduce the party, as two portable cookers would not be enough for six men of his party. "I had no alternative but to send Jack, Gaze and Cope back to the base at Cape Evans and carry on south with Richards, Hayward and the four dogs," Joyce wrote.

Joyce's team pulled almost 1,400 pounds on the sledge, and covered ten miles per day, which Joyce called "quite satisfactory travelling." On January 18, at 82 degrees they met Mackintosh, Wild and Spencer-Smith, who was showing signs of scurvy. "This was most unfortunate," Joyce wrote, "because we had not finished our task, upon which Shackleton's party depended for their lives."

On January 21 they reached 83 degrees, with the foot of the Beardmore Glacier, the planned site of the southernmost depot, only 35 miles away. With Spencer-Smith's health failing, they left him alone in a tent and hurried to reach their final destination. They laid the depot at Mount Hope, near the base of the glacier, on January 26. Despite bitter cold, illness, a lack of supplies and a shortage of dogs, they had accomplished their goal. When Shackleton and his men descended the Beardmore, the depots would be there to provide the essential food and fuel that would keep them alive. Mackintosh was pleased, but it was also now quite apparent that he, too, was suffering from scurvy. Hut Point, and safety, was four hundred miles away.

Chapter 22 Leadership Concept:

Combine Resourcefulness, Optimism & Focus: Mackintosh helped keep his stranded men optimistic by explaining to them what they would need to do to survive, and by keeping them focused on the tasks at hand.

Chapter 23

The Men Who Did Not Fail

On January 29 the Depot Party reached Spencer-Smith's tent to find him still alive, but unable to walk. The ailing vicar was placed on a sledge and dragged by his companions. At first the team did well, averaging between fifteen and eighteen miles per day, but when they were about two miles from Scott's burial cairn a vicious blizzard began, confining the party to their tent. After a week in the tent living on half-rations, Joyce decided they would have to resume the march, as the men were getting weaker, and there was only one day's worth of dog food left.

Due to their weakened condition, it took them three hours to load the sledge, and when Spencer-Smith was placed aboard he fell into unconsciousness. As they trudged north, sixty mile per hour winds tore at the men and the dogs. Only five minutes into the march, Mackintosh collapsed. Joyce consulted with Wild, Richards and Hayward. It would be impossible to pull both sick men, so they decided to leave Wild behind to care for Mackintosh and Spencer-Smith, while the other three made a dash for the next depot, eleven miles north. They left what little food they had with Wild. Joyce was reluctant to leave anyone behind, but he had little choice. "Richards, Hayward and I turned away, and urging on our four dogs, faced the north, where there was food. Not once did we look back after leaving Wild, but every step was an effort of will, every yard a torture." In fourteen hours they covered less than four miles. Each man ate just one quarter of a biscuit. The dogs did not eat at all.

After a miserable, freezing night they struggled forward the next day for fifteen hours, gaining four miles, "until it seemed that life was just one painful step after another," Joyce wrote. The dogs went a second day without food. "Their wistful look touched me so that I had to go out and pet them." By the third day, the men and dogs of Joyce's party were nearing the end. "Just a couple of miles to the east of us my old chief, Captain Scott, and his companions were sleeping peacefully under the snow," Joyce recalled.

Although besieged by a blizzard, the trio pushed forward. "We stumbled, we lurched, we halted in our step, but we never stopped," Joyce wrote. On the fourth day, Richards spotted the depot. The dogs ran to it, but it took the men hours to cover the two hundred yards between themselves and life sustaining food. "I can only say it was a miracle that we saw the flag," Joyce wrote. "To pick up a cairn in a blizzard is like picking up a buoy in the Atlantic in a snowstorm."

After setting up the tent, the men first attended to feeding the dogs, but the animals resisted and only "nosed round" the food. The men did the same, wisely eating only small amounts at first. They had gone eight days with barely any food.

After two days of rest, the men were strong enough to begin the rescue of Wild, Mackintosh, and Spencer-Smith. They loaded the sledge with food, but the dogs refused to pull south. Joyce fooled the dogs by starting them off north, then making a wide turn. Hayward, also suffering from scurvy, became too weak to walk and was placed on the sledge. On February 28, an ailing Mackintosh penned a farewell letter, but it was premature as Joyce's team reached them the next day.

On the first of March they resumed the trek north, dragging Mackintosh, Hayward and Spencer-Smith on the sledge. With the wind at their backs they made good time the first day, but when the breeze abandoned them they were left with mere pulling power, and that was not enough. "I discovered that under these circumstances we were covering only 100 yards in five hours," Joyce wrote. "I put it to two of the invalids, Mackintosh and Hayward, that one of them would have to remain on the Barrier." They knew Spencer-Smith's only chance at survival was to get to fresh meat as soon as possible. Mackintosh volunteered to stay behind. "It was a brave act, for to be left there in that howling, frozen wilderness, and with very little will to live, is the greatest test of a man's courage and endurance," Joyce wrote.

The party, without Mackintosh, went forward. At night they tied pieces of bamboo to Spencer-Smith's legs to keep them straight. Despite their best efforts, especially the unceasing care provided by Ernie Wild, Reverend Spencer-Smith died on March 9, eight days before his 32nd birthday. "It was a great blow to us when Spencer-Smith died. We were only nineteen miles from the base and had had great hopes of getting him in," Joyce wrote. Spencer-Smith had been ill for fifty-four days, and Joyce and his team had carried him on the sledge for forty-four. "To lose him so near to our journey's end was heartbreaking. All through that terrible time of trial he showed the greatest fortitude, and the epitaph which I gave him on the cross erected on the snow-cairn grave was just this, 'A Brave Man.' That simple wording described him absolutely."

By this point, all the men were suffering from scurvy and snow blindness, but they finally arrived at Hut Point. On March 14, after regaining their strength, Joyce, Wild, and Richards left Hayward in the Hut and returned, with the dogs, to rescue Mackintosh, whom they reached on March 16. To their surprise and joy, he was still alive. By the 18th they had returned to the Terra Nova Hut at Hut Point, where they would have to wait until the sea ice became hard enough to cross before reaching their crewmates and the better conditions at the Discovery Hut at Cape Evans. Joyce calculated that by this point they had marched 200 days and over 1900 miles.

Superlative efforts by the remaining dogs had helped them survive this final journey. "I have no hesitation in saying that but for them we should never have got through to safety," Joyce wrote. "For more than 200 days they worked with a will and came through all that fearful weather and we had no mushing-whip! Their only spur was kind words."

The ice that had held the *Aurora* for so many months began to loosen in February, and leads finally opened on March 1st. The ship, battered and bruised by the pressure of the ice, now had numerous leaks which required constant pumping. Stenhouse steered the ship through pack ice and around large bergs, and finally cleared the last belt of ice on March 14. The *Aurora* made wireless contact on March 23, and was met by a tug on April 2. The next day the damaged vessel, which had survived powerful storms and crushing ice, limped into Port Chalmers, New Zealand.

Five men were at the Terra Nova Hut at Hut Point: Mackintosh, Wild, Joyce, Richards, and Hayward, waiting for the thirteen miles of sea ice to thicken so they could cross to the Discovery Hut at Cape Evans. Mackintosh surprised Joyce by announcing that he and Hayward, both now recuperated from scurvy, were going to make the crossing. Joyce warned the Captain against the journey, noting that the ice, though possibly firm enough to cross, was still unstable and could be blown out to sea by a storm at any moment. Mackintosh would not be dissuaded, however, and he and Hayward left camp without a tent, sleeping bags, or any other emergency gear. A storm began soon after their departure. On May 10, Joyce and Richards followed the footsteps of the Mackintosh and Hayward until they came to an abrupt end. There was no way of knowing if the two men had successfully crossed the ice.

In mid-July, Joyce, Richards and Wild crossed the ice between Hut Point and Cape Evans. They had hoped to travel under the light of a full moon, but a lunar eclipse obscured much of the illumination. On July 15, they arrived at Cape Evans, and were met by the barking of dogs, including several who had been born in Antarctica. The fur of the dogs was bathed in a prism of colors as the light of the moon returned.

Joyce was relieved to find that Stevens, Cope, Gaze and Jack were all well. There was a brief, joyous reunion, but it was quickly tempered by the realization that Mackintosh and Hayward had never arrived. There was also great concern for Stenhouse and the crew of the *Aurora*, which they presumed had been lost, and for Shackleton and his men, who had never appeared from the South.

Gaze and Jack used their time at Cape Evans to construct a cross to place at the grave of Gaze's cousin, Spencer-Smith. In mid-December, Joyce, Wild and Gaze returned the Barrier, and located the gravesite. There they erected the cross, which held a simple inscription: "Sacred to the memory of Rev. A.P. Spencer-Smith, who died 9 March 1916. A brave man." They returned to the Terra Nova Hut in the beginning of January and resumed the routine of hunting for seals to extend their meager food supply.

On the morning of January 10, 1917, Richards glanced towards the water, and spotted movement in the distance. He returned to the Hut and quietly stated that a ship had arrived to rescue them. The other men, having just finished eating breakfast, took his remark as a bad joke and ignored him. When Richards persuaded them to see for themselves, the excitement began.

Sea ice prevented the ship from reaching the men, so they sledged onto the ice. As they moved closer they saw black specks coming towards them, which turned out to be three men, including Shackleton. After the initial handshakes, Shackleton learned of the loss of Mackintosh, Hayward and Spencer-Smith. Shackleton and his two companions laid down on the ice as a signal to the ship of how many men were lost.

Before leaving for New Zealand, Shackleton searched for the bodies of Mackintosh and Hayward, but to no avail. Wild and Jack built a cross at the base of Mt. Erebus in honor the fallen members of the Ross Sea Party. *Aurora* left Antarctica on January 17, and docked in Wellington on February 9th, 1917. Shackleton's ambitious plan, the Imperial Trans-Antarctic Expedition, had finally ended.

Joyce wrote: "Strung out on the Great Ice Barrier the chain of depots still stretches for 360 miles to Mount Hope, holding their food rations, perhaps to save the lives of future explorers, perhaps only as a memorial, unseen by man, to the faithfulness of the men who did not fail."

Chapter 23 Leadership Concept:

The Power of Responsibility: With Mackintosh ill, leadership fell to Joyce, who guided a team of men, some extremely debilitated, on a selfless 2,000 mile trek. Joyce did everything humanly possible to meet the dual and conflicting goals of keeping his men alive while also laying the precious depots for Shackleton. His powerful sense of responsibility, empathy, and indomitable will guided his decision making and leadership.

Chapter 24

Facing South

When Shackleton, Worsley and Crean reached the whaling station in South Georgia on May 20, 1916, the Boss asked how long the war had been over. The fighting, of course, was far from finished, and for the first time the three explorers heard about the unprecedented magnitude of death and destruction that had taken place. They were forced to absorb in one conversation what the rest of world had learned in stages over almost two years. "We were like men arisen from the dead to a world gone mad, and it took our minds some time to accustom themselves to the tales of nations in arms, of deathless courage and unimagined slaughter...No other civilized men could have been as blankly ignorant of world-shaking events as we were," Shackleton recalled.

The crew of the *Endurance* had survived the loss of their ship, the harsh environment of Elephant Island, and the perils of the Southern Ocean, but the world they were returning to was far more dangerous than anything they had encountered beneath the Antarctic Circle. No longer protected by the icy isolation they had longed to escape, Shackleton's men were exposed to the harsh realities of the First World War.

Timothy McCarthy, who had endured the journey of the *James Caird* and impressed Shackleton and Worsley with his irrepressible optimism, was killed in action in the English

Channel in March, 1917, his first day in combat. McCarthy was the first member of the *Endurance* crew to die. He was twenty-eight years old.

Frank Wild's brother Ernie, who had cared so diligently for the ailing Spencer-Smith during the *Aurora's* depot laying journeys, died on a mine-sweeper in the Mediterranean.

Antarctic veteran Alf Cheetham returned home from the *Endurance* expedition to the tragic news that his son Alfred, one of thirteen children, had died in the war while the elder Cheetham was returning from Antarctica. Alf Cheetham joined the merchant marine, and was himself killed when his ship, the SS *Prunelle* was torpedoed by a German U boat in late August 1918, less than three months before the armistice. Alf Cheetham was fifty-one. Other members of the *Endurance* and *Aurora* crews were badly injured during the war, including McIlroy, the surgeon, and Wordie, the geologist.

Not surprisingly, many crewmembers of the *Endurance* demonstrated the same courage and resourcefulness during the war that they had shown in the Antarctic. Macklin won the Military Cross for aiding wounded men under fire on the Italian front, while Stenhouse and Worsley proved highly adept at destroying German submarines. Worsley even picked up the nickname "Depth-Charge Bill." Frank Wild served with distinction in the North Russian front, while Hussey distinguished himself in some of the bloodiest battles of the war.

Shackleton was sent by the British government to South America to drum up support for the Allied cause, then to Northern Russia, where he was in charge of Arctic Equipment and Transport. For a time Wild, Worsley, Stenhouse, Hussey and Macklin were with him, and Shackleton was proud of the work they did on the Murmansk front. "The mobile columns there had exactly the same clothing, equipment and sledging food as we had on the Expedition. No expense was spared to get the best of everything for them, and consequently not a single case of avoidable frost-bite was reported," he recalled.

After the war, Shackleton made plans for a return to Antarctica, and secured enough funds from childhood friend John Quiller Rowatt to finance a journey aboard the *Quest*, a small Norwegian sealer. Shackleton met with Worsley in London and asked him to join the venture. When Worsley advised the Boss that he had started his own company and was not in a financial position to leave, Shackleton paid Worsley's debts, freeing the Skipper to join the expedition. Worsley was pleased to find out that several members of the *Endurance* crew, including Wild, Macklin, Green, and Hussey, had already accepted Shackleton's offer to return to the Antarctic.

The *Quest* departed London, sailing down the River Thames, on September 18, 1921. Other ships sounded their whistles, celebrating the ship and its legendary commander. After a few stops, the *Quest* arrived in Rio de Janeiro on November 21st. The ship's engines were failing and had to be repaired, which caused a one month delay. Shackleton was dismayed, as he did not want to lose a crucial summer month in Antarctica. In December, while still in Rio, Shackleton suffered a heart attack. He recovered, and though he was in a weakened condition, the *Quest* sailed for South Georgia on December 18. During the voyage, Shackleton often stayed in his cabin, which he made sure provided no items or comforts not given to the crew. Worsley noticed that Shackleton was unusually nostalgic.

On Christmas Day, as the *Quest* was nearing South Georgia, a hurricane began, tossing the small vessel around in the rough seas. Only Worsley's technique of spreading oil on top of the water stopped the waves from breaking over the ship, but the *Quest* still developed a crack in the boiler and a leak in the fresh water tank. On January 4, 1922, The *Quest* docked at South Georgia, and Shackleton displayed renewed energy. He was excited to return to the location of one of his great successes, and was eager to point out where he, Worsley, and Crean had careened down the mountainside years earlier. That night, Shackleton and Worsley sat in the Boss' cabin and discussed their plans. Shackleton asked Worsley if he would like to lead a sledging expedition into uncharted areas, and promised the Skipper that he could name any new lands he discovered. Worsley was tremendously impressed by Shackleton's generosity.

During the night, Shackleton suffered another heart attack. He called for Dr. Macklin, but there was nothing the physician could do. Shackleton jokingly asked "I wonder what you'll cut me off from doing after this, Mac?" A few minutes later, Shackleton was dead. Emily suggested he be buried on South Georgia, the place that symbolized his single greatest achievement, saving the crew of the *Endurance*. Every crewmember of the *Quest* helped build a stone cairn in his honor, but unlike all other graves on South Georgia, Shackleton's was dug facing south.

Chapter 25

N25

The arrival of the *Quest*, without Shackleton, in Plymouth on September 16, 1922 marked the end of the Heroic Age of Antarctic Exploration. To accurately judge Roald Amundsen's leadership in its entirety, however, we must expand the scope of our research beyond the Heroic Age, and to the opposite end of the earth.

Following his triumphant attainment of the South Pole, Amundsen penned his story, *Sydpolen* (*The South Pole*), and conducted a lecture tour of Europe and the United States. By July 1914, he was preparing to guide the *Fram* north, hoping to recreate Nansen's journey of 1893-1896, which used the clockwise drift of Arctic Sea ice to travel close to the North Pole. Whereas Shackleton had been given approval to proceed south despite the onset of World War I, the *Fram* expedition was cancelled, and Amundsen's return to the Arctic was postponed.

Norway's neutrality and location created opportunities for profit during the war, and Amundsen's financial situation, always in flux, was soon riding a wave of prosperity. He used much of his earnings on a new ship, the *Maud*, to replace the aging *Fram,* and in July 1918 Amundsen left Norway in his new vessel. Amundsen named Helmer Hanssen, who had served aboard the *Gjoa* and later been part of the South Pole team, as captain.

The *Maud* was trapped in ice for three winters, and during this time the relationship between Amundsen and Hanssen began to break down. Hanssen was dismissed when the ship reached Nome, Alaska, ending an eighteen year relationship between the two men. Although the expedition failed to reach the North Pole, important scientific data was gathered by geophysicist Harald Sverdrup.

A second attempt, which ended in 1925, also failed. The two unsuccessful voyages reversed Amundsen's fortunes, and the *Maud* was sold to the Hudson Bay Company to help satisfy creditors. Amundsen was lecturing to generate income, but it was far too little to make a dent in his debts. He calculated that he would have to live to one hundred and ten to pay off his creditors and make another attempt at the Pole.

Amundsen's fortunes changed dramatically when he received a call from wealthy American Lincoln Ellsworth, who agreed to support future expeditions with the caveat that he be included on them. Amundsen, with a renewed spirit, proposed a new plan: fly two planes from King's Bay, West Spitsbergen to the North Pole and back. Two seaplanes, *N24* and *N25*, were purchased and shipped to Spitsbergen, where they were assembled and test flown.

On May 21, 1925, the planes began their mission. Amundsen's crew, aboard *N25*, included Royal Norwegian Navy Lieutenant Hjalmar Riiser-Larsen and German mechanic Karl Feucht. The *N24* was manned by Ellsworth and Naval Lieutenants Oskar Omdal and Leif Dietrichson, whom Amundsen relied on for his skill as a pilot and his positive outlook.

The pilots had planned to keep the planes near each other, and after a brief separation early on they managed to stay close despite a heavy fog. The planes emerged from the haze well to the west of their intended position, then steered eastward and hoped for the best. After ten hours, half the fuel was gone, and it was decided to seek out a possible landing area. Ice was preferred over water, as ice might close in on an area of open water and crush the plane. Riiser-Larsen executed a difficult landing, but lost sight of *N24*.

Amundsen now turned *N25* from aircraft to shelter. One section was determined to be optimal for dining and sleeping, and the Primus stove was set up there. On May 23, two days after takeoff, Amundsen clamored to the top of *N25* with his binoculars, and from there spotted *N24*. On May 26 Amundsen watched as the crew of *N24* attempted to cross the ice towards him. The men battled icebergs and fissures, and used a small canvas boat to traverse open areas of water. Amundsen watched as the crew disappeared behind an iceberg, and when he heard yelling he knew the men were in trouble. As the cries lessened Amundsen feared the worst, but to his great relief all three men soon appeared, alive and well. Dietrichson had plunged through the ice, followed almost immediately by Omdal. Ellsworth hauled Dietrichson out, and together they had saved Omdal.

Dietrichson informed Amundsen that *N24* had been damaged and would not be able to make a return trip. All six men now took up lodging in *N25*, which had landed in a slushy mix of water and ice that was not particularly stable. Amundsen, Riiser-Larsen and Feucht had been unable to move the aircraft, but with the additional manpower of Dietrichson, Omdal and Ellsworth, *N25* was quickly transferred to a safer location.

With the plane secured, Amundsen set his mind to their escape. Fuel was obtained from *N24*, providing enough for a return trip to Spitsbergen. Food, however, was scarce. They were limited to what little food they had brought with them, as there were no seals, polar bears, or other game to be found. The men were forced to survive on meager rations.

The challenge facing the cold, weakened crew would be to create a flat, thirteen hundred foot runway necessary for takeoff. *N25* was moved to a large ice floe, and the men began the painstaking work of constructing a viable surface. The tools they had with them were not designed for this type of work—a few knives, an axe, and an ice-anchor that could serve as a pick. Improvised tools proved very useful, as Omdal broke up ice with the iron-bound bottom of their camera tripod.

On the night of June 2, *N25* nearly suffered the same fate as the *Endurance*. At midnight the men were awoken by Amundsen's shouts that the plane was being crushed. All provisions were quickly removed, and the crew rocked the *N25* enough to let the ice close in underneath the plane without destroying it.

There was an alternative to flying back—the men could man-haul their provisions on the sledge towards Greenland. A vote was held— Riiser-Larsen voted for walking, while Feucht opted for the plane. Omdal stated he would follow the majority vote, and Ellsworth stated he wanted to wait before deciding. Amundsen had told them that by June 15 they would have to make a final choice either way. To leave any later would mean there would not be enough food left to get them to Greenland.

At first Amundsen leaned towards man-hauling, reasoning that even if their supplies ran out they might be able to hunt for food farther south. The plane option, though, was too appealing to ignore. If the flight went well, they could be safely back in civilization in eight hours. Amundsen voted for the plane.

The men worked tirelessly to build the runway, which they completed on June 14, only one day before the deadline. Amundsen had established a strict schedule for work, sleep, and meals which kept them focused and optimistic. Ellsworth estimated they had moved 300 tons of snow, while Amundsen suggested 500 tons. Either way, it was a Herculean effort on one half pound of food per day. On the night of June 15 the temperature dipped enough to solidify the runway, and a slight wind from the southeast emerged. At 10:30 p.m. they prepared for takeoff. The plane and the runway did their job. Soon *N25* was airborne, and Amundsen's men were on their way home. After spotting a ship near Nordostland, a Norwegian island, *N25* performed a water landing.

Amundsen and the men of *N25* returned to Norway as heroes. On July 5, 1925, *N25* flew over the capital to the cheers of thousands of spectators, then landed in the water amidst numerous boats that joined in the celebration. The crew was honored at a reception in the presence of Norwegian royals.

Amundsen and Ellsworth enjoyed the celebrations but were already focused on another attempt at the Pole. Their revised plan was to traverse the Arctic by flying from Svalbard, a Norwegian archipelago, to Alaska, thus becoming the first people to fly over the North Pole. Instead of using a plane they decided on the airship *Norge*, which had been constructed in Italy, designed by Colonel Umberto Nobile. The expedition was financially supported by Ellsworth and the Italian government of Benito Mussolini.

Amundsen and Ellsworth met the Colonel in Rome and then flew north in the *Norge* with Nobile as pilot. On May 2, 1926 the three were in Russia when they learned that American Richard Byrd had arrived in King's Bay with a Fokker monoplane on his ship, the *Chantier*. The *Norge* flew into King's Bay early in the morning of May 7. From the air Amundsen saw the *Chantier*, and Byrd's plane, the *Josephine Ford*.

The *Norge* was brought into a hangar that had been built specifically for it, and final preparations for the polar flight began. A damaged engine had to be replaced, and Nobile told Amundsen and Ellsworth it would take three days to make the *Norge* ready for flight.

Nobile also mentioned that the work could be sped up if they wanted to get airborne before Byrd, but Amundsen replied that while Byrd was racing for the Pole, his plan was to cross the Arctic, and flying over the Pole was only part of that journey. It was decided to continue on as planned, preparing steadily without rushing. Byrd and the Americans, meanwhile, worked quickly, by the early morning of May 9 the Fokker was ready.

At 1:50 a.m. Amundsen and his men were awakened by the sound of the Fokker's powerful engine. They ran outside in time to see the monoplane take off. By 5 p.m. Byrd and pilot Floyd Bennett had returned. When the plane landed, Amundsen and Ellsworth were among the first to congratulate Byrd.

It was a series of events eerily similar to the South Pole race, with Amundsen now cast in the role of Scott. Amundsen's desire to be the first man to fly over the North Pole had been subverted by a rival who had captured the prize using a more efficient method of travel. Like Scott, Amundsen had decided not to alter his plans just to win the race, and stated that the goal of his expedition was broader than simply being first to the Pole.

On May 11, 1926, the *Norge* began its journey northward with a crew that included Amundsen, Ellsworth, Nobile, and Oscar Wisting, a member of Amundsen's Polar Party from 1911. As the *Norge* passed over the top of the Earth, Amundsen and Wisting, the first two people to reach both of the Earth's poles, shook hands.

Byrd's achievement was not without controversy. The accomplishment was impossible to prove, and the debate over the authenticity of Byrd's claim has gone on for decades. If Byrd did not actually reach the Pole, as some evidence suggests, then Amundsen's remarkable legacy also includes being the first explorer to soar over the North Pole.

On May 14 the *Norge* set down safely near Nome. The expedition had been a successful combination of American, Norwegian and Italian efforts, but it soon became clear that infighting had occurred between Nobile and Amundsen. Nobile viewed himself as Amundsen's equal, while to Amundsen Nobile was merely an airship pilot.

Amundsen retired after the *Norge* journey, wrote a bitter autobiography, and began to act increasingly odd, as if the years of Polar toil had taken a cumulative mental toll. But Amundsen, who had achieved more in the polar regions than anyone, was destined not to fade into obscurity sitting out his remaining years at home.

In 1928 Nobile returned to the Arctic for further exploration in the semi-dirigible *Italia*. On May 25, radio contact was lost, and the crew of the *Italia* was feared dead. Mussolini refused numerous offers of international assistance to provide search and rescue missions. On June 7, radio signals were finally picked up. The ship had crashed, six crewmen were dead, but there were survivors, including Nobile, stranded on an ice floe. The rescue missions no longer waited for Mussolini's approval. Amundsen procured a plane and left Tromso, Norway on June 18, 1928, with five crewmen. Among the crew was *N25* veteran Leif Dietrichson, whose skill and cheerful outlook

Amundsen so admired. Tragically, Amundsen's plane disappeared with all hands. Nobile and the other survivors of the *Italia* crash were eventually rescued by a Swedish pilot.

Searches now began for Amundsen's plane. Tryggve Gran, the Norwegian member of Scott's *Terra Nova* expedition, now an officer in the Royal Norwegian Air Force, commanded one of the search teams. Pieces of the plane were found, but the bodies were never recovered. Amundsen, like Scott, Wilson, Shackleton and others who had accomplished their greatest achievements in the polar regions, would spend eternity there.

Chapter 25 Leadership Concept:

The Power of Scheduling: Just as Shackleton had done, Amundsen made sure his stranded men were as happy and focused as possible while they created a runway for the *N25*. Amundsen established and enforced a strict routine for the men to follow. Work, sleep, and meals were scheduled, and the six men lived harmoniously and were highly productive during the twenty-five days they were trapped on the ice.

Chapter 26

The Antarctic Model of Leadership

Like many things, leadership is a combination of both common sense and complex concepts. If we focus too much on the common sense aspect, we may overlook important techniques and subtleties that are not apparent at first glance. However, if we delve too deeply into theory, or try to utilize overly elaborate models, we can lose sight of the efficiency that is required for effective, real-time leadership. Our goal is a practical model with a strong foundation based on the in-depth study of actual events.

Leadership has been studied for decades, primarily in academia, the business world, or by the military. Dozens of theories and models have emerged, with many touted as *the* concept that finally explains what makes great leaders. Leadership, however, is a complicated and somewhat amorphous entity, and as we continue to study it we should remain open to new ideas and innovative research that further our understanding and enable more people to become effective leaders. This model, consisting of seven key concepts and rooted in the actual experiences of Antarctic commanders, is presented as part of that ongoing process.

Concept 1: Vision, Decision, & Precision

Effective leaders need to dream big, make the crucial decision to turn their visions into reality, then focus intensely on the details necessary for success. Shackleton, Scott, Amundsen and Mawson all shared the ability to visualize and actualize enormous expeditions, involving people, animals, financing, ships, equipment, food and supplies, then focus on the day-to-day particulars of getting the job done.

Nansen spent a lifetime turning ideas into tangible successes. Not only was he able to conceptualize the crossing of Greenland and the attempt at the North Pole, but he took the key next step of bringing his ideas to fruition. Later, as an international diplomat, he solved immense global problems using the same process.

Concept 2: Harness the Power of Planning and the Acquisition of Knowledge

Amundsen was by far the most successful of the polar explorers. His prodigious accomplishments were directly related to his dedication to preparation, which included detailed planning and the constant attainment of useful information. As a teenager he had the foresight to begin a rigorous training program of long distance skiing to prepare himself for a career in polar exploration that was years away. As one of the pioneering sailors of the Heroic Age aboard the *Belgica*, he learned how to defeat cold, scurvy, boredom and man-hauling, the banes of Antarctic exploration. Amundsen obtained practical skills from the Netsilik during his stay at Gjoa Haven in the Arctic, making him the most knowledgeable Polar explorer in the world. He coupled this expertise with precise preparation that allowed him to attain the South Pole with remarkable ease.

Lack of preparation, conversely, had tragic results in the unforgiving Polar environments. Antarctica wasted little time educating Scott and the *Discovery* crew about the hazards of bringing insufficient knowledge and lack of experience to an extremely dangerous situation, resulting in the loss of Vince. Similarly, Wiik's tragic death aboard the *Gjoa* might have been avoided had a physician been aboard, and Amundsen's failure to include a ship's surgeon among the crew is surprising and inexcusable. An effective leader must be sure that his or her team is prepared to deal with adverse conditions and changing situations.

Concept 3: Select a Multitalented Team that is Task Specific

Amundsen assembled a crew specifically designed to win the race to the South Pole. The men were first rate dog team drivers, skiers, carpenters and navigators—the exact skills required for success. Significantly, each man was multitalented. Hansen and Hassel were both expert dog team drivers and top flight navigators, while Bjaaland was a talented carpenter and a first rate skier. Amundsen's highly skilled, well equipped party showed what can be accomplished by a team operating at top efficiency. They turned what had been a nightmarish struggle for survival for other explorers into a relatively easy attainment of and return from the South Pole.

Shackleton selected the crew of the *Endurance* from over five thousand applicants, looking for highly motivated, talented individualists who could also be team players. He showed that through a shrewd and thorough selection process, you can find skilled, unique individuals who can function as a cohesive unit even in dire circumstances.

Concept 4: Build Trust and Loyalty by Putting Your People First

With the team in place, an effective leader must inspire trust and loyalty by giving top priority to the needs of their people. The Antarctic commanders demonstrated this in a variety of ways.

Selflessness: Shackleton's act of giving his food to Frank Wild, and the loyalty Wild felt in return, exemplifies how leaders can foster devotion through selflessness. In spite of the bitter cold and terrible hunger he had endured, Wild agreed to return to the Antarctic with Shackleton without hesitation. Similarly, Scott's act of saving the two dogs from a crevasse, and his refusal to let anyone else attempt such a dangerous task, demonstrated his unselfishness, kindness, and bravery. Scott would not ask anyone to take a risk in his place. These qualities inspired the same type of trust and loyalty in Wilson that Wild felt for Shackleton.

The Good of the Men: Both Scott and Shackleton were desperate to reach the South Pole, but neither was willing to sacrifice the safety of their men to achieve their goal. The lives of each of his men meant more to Scott and Shackleton than anything else, and their men knew it. During the return trip from the South Pole, Scott refused to abandon the ailing Evans or Oates, at tremendous risk to himself.

Fairness: With food scarce, Shackleton put procedures in place to ensure that every man in the Southern Party felt he was being given equal rations. This evenhandedness prevented the bitterness and anger that even a hint of inequality would have caused. Shackleton made sure that his policy of equal treatment was evident. He ate the same food and lived in the same conditions as his men.

When Amundsen reached the South Pole, he made sure that each member of his party grasped the flagpole as they planted it in the ice. Each crewman was able to share equally in the glory of the achievement. The egalitarianism and sacrifice shown by the commanders went a long way towards earning the trust and respect of their crews. Even under mundane conditions, employees desire fairness and expect equal treatment from management.

Concept 5: Manage Strategically

After trust and loyalty have been established, an effective leader still has to manage skillfully and strategically to help the team reach its full potential.

Vest Individuals in the Team's Success. Amundsen kept his crews small, and gave each crew member multiple responsibilities. This served two key purposes. First, it kept them busy during the long, cold months of isolation and darkness. Second, it gave each man a powerful feeling of being an indispensable member of the team whose performance was vital to the success of the mission. This sense of importance made each man view the team's success as his own.

Deal With Serious Issues Quickly. When food was stolen on Elephant Island, Wild made it clear that any recurrence would be dealt with severely. His prompt response ended what would certainly have become a cause of dissension among the crew. Wild also settled petty differences and kept the men on Elephant Island as positive as possible considering the gravity of their situation.

Remove Divisiveness from the Team. Amundsen quickly banished Johansen from the Polar Party after the veteran explorer confronted him. Although his treatment of Johansen and the others was harsh, once this internal conflict had emerged it had to be dealt with immediately. Amundsen would not allow any discord that would distract the team during their dash to the Pole. Similarly, Shackleton quickly quieted

McNeish's rebellion to the agonizing process of relaying sledges across the ice.

Make the practical, not the popular choice: When the *Endurance* crew spotted land after months of tedious drifting on the ice, they were understandably anxious to take to the boats and begin rowing. Shackleton's decision to wait until they were beyond dangerous pack ice was cautious and pragmatic. A leader more concerned with his popularity might have given in to the crew's emotions and made a rash but dangerous decision.

Be Clear When Delegating Authority: Shackleton's orders to Joyce and Mackintosh were vague and overlapping. This led to disagreements, compromises, and poor decisions that could likely have been avoided with more definitive charges.

Admit Your Mistakes: Shackleton acknowledged to Worsley that he had been wrong about the amount of ballast that should be used on the *Caird*—which only further impressed the Captain about Shackleton's character.

Keep Your Sense of Humor: Even in the most trying of circumstances, Shackleton would joke with his men, helping to keep their spirits up.

Make Sure Your People are Ready for the Task Ahead: Amundsen kept the men of the *Fram* busy, happy, and as comfortable as possible while they waited out the winter. Each crewman was given specific, important duties to focus on. Amundsen wanted them mentally and physically healthy for the push to the Pole. Scott, conversely, allowed Wilson and Bowers, key members of his team, to undertake an exhausting, dangerous, and unnecessary mission to a penguin rookery during the dead of winter, weakening them for the upcoming race.

Concept 6: Lead by Example and Persevere

Although Scott's reliance on man-hauling seems impractical when compared with Amundsen's efficiency, it cannot be overlooked that Scott and his team reached the South Pole—and had enough food stored to return safely—using man-hauling as their primary form of transportation. They demonstrated that with extreme effort, determination, and perseverance, almost anything can be accomplished. Scott worked as hard as any member of the team, which increased their devotion to him and their commitment to the mission. The men serving under him never failed to give their all even in the most dire circumstances. Scott also showed great empathy for the men and dogs who toiled and suffered on his expeditions.

With Mackintosh ill, leadership of the Ross Sea Party fell to Joyce, one of the truly unsung heroes of Antarctic exploration. Joyce led a team that toiled untiringly to meet the dual yet conflicting goals of keeping his men alive while also laying the precious depots for Shackleton. Although Joyce didn't have the glory of attaining the Pole as an incentive, his party sledged almost 2,000 miles purely to save the lives of their fellow explorers.

Considering the failure of the dog teams and the effect scurvy had on the men, it is remarkable that Scott, Wilson and Shackleton made it as far south as they did, and returned alive during the *Discovery* expedition. While their planning was suspect, their resolve, both individually and as a team, carried them to unprecedented achievement.

Mawson's story, besides graphically depicting the perils of Antarctic exploration, rivals any tale of perseverance. Mawson demonstrated what can be accomplished through tenacious effort and the will to survive. When leaders in more mundane situations face serious problems or tough choices, they would be wise to think of Mawson, who literally pulled himself out of the abyss.

Concept 7: Use an Understanding of Human Psychology to Constantly Improve Morale

Use Structure and Personal Communication: If Amundsen exemplified the power of preparation, Shackleton typified a leader who understood his crew's psychology and the importance of maintaining high morale. With the crew of the *Endurance* stranded on the ice, Shackleton worked tirelessly to keep them optimistic, entertained, and focused. His technique of using frequent personal communication, speaking to people individually or in small groups, allowed him to gauge morale and impart his optimism. Except for the period in which he suffered from a debilitating bout of sciatica, Shackleton visited each tent daily, meeting with his men personally. He used humor, organized activities, and a rotation of duties and tent assignments to keep the crew focused and upbeat. Shackleton also looked for opportunities to heighten morale. The ascension of Mt. Erebus during the *Nimrod* expedition, for example, lifted the spirits of the entire crew.

Other commanders used similar methods with equal success. The unheralded Campbell accomplished a remarkable feat of leadership by keeping the men of the Northern Party alive and hopeful during their torturous stay on Inexpressible Island. Campbell used songs, stories, routine, and a contagious positive outlook. Amundsen established and enforced a strict schedule of work, rest and meals to keep the men of *N25* content and focused during the Herculean task of building a runway on the ice.

Each of these leaders managed to keep the spirits of their crews up, even in the face of the most calamitous conditions. In contrast, early Heroic Age commanders Borchgrevink and de Gerlache discovered how easily morale can plummet if a leader does not take an active, daily role in improving it.

Be Selective When Disseminating Information:
Shackleton knew that maintaining morale was a top priority, and found additional ways to keep spirits high besides establishing routine and spreading his infectious optimism through personal communication. He was careful to only disseminate information as needed, so as not to upset the crew unnecessarily. When he realized the *Endurance* would ultimately be crushed, he shared this information only with his top confidants, Wild and Worsley. This allowed the crew to remain happier for a long period of time, and not worry unnecessarily about something they had no control over.

Shackleton used a similar technique when the boat crews were rowing for Elephant Island. Despite hard rowing by the crew under terrible circumstances, the winds and current had actually pushed the small boats thirty miles farther away from their destination. Shackleton wisely mitigated the damage this news would have had on the crew's morale, telling them only that their progress had been less than expected.

Shackleton had a keen understanding of human psychology, and used it effectively as a leader. He was quick to spot men in trouble and help them, but without singling individuals out. While camped on the ice, he would rotate tent assignments on pretext, often bringing men who needed the most attention into his own tent, while never giving away the real reason for the move. During the terrible voyage of the *James Caird*, Shackleton would order hot drinks for everyone when one man was getting too cold, thus keeping up the confidence of each individual and maintaining the group's morale.

Applying the Model

We often hear that "leadership starts at the top," and logic indicates this maxim to be true. If the owner of a baseball franchise doesn't care if their team wins the World Series, that owner won't invest money in the players the team needs to win. It is essential for an effective leader to aim high, to *want* their organization to reach its full potential. If leaders at all levels are actively working in this direction, then there truly is an opportunity for the organization to be the best it can be.

Once high expectations have been set, it is vital that the leader be able to marry that vision to a plan of action—the method of achieving the goal. The key elements at this stage are thorough planning, acquiring the necessary knowledge needed to be successful in a given field, and a keen attention to detail.

With the plan in place, the next step is building a multitalented team of individuals with job specific skills who can work cohesively. Assembling the right group is a crucial element of effective leadership. Even the most visionary owner and shrewdest manager will win nothing without the right players on the field.

After amassing a quality team, an effective leader must inspire trust, loyalty and confidence through selflessness, fairness, and putting their people above their own desires or ambitions. With this trust in place, an effective leader has the opportunity to manage tactically, by handling serious issues quickly, removing potential divisiveness, and being clear when delegating authority. A trusted leader can make practical, if not always popular decisions, and still retain the respect of their people. Effective leaders also make sure their people are mentally and physically ready to perform whatever tasks are necessary, and that they have the tools they need to do the job.

Successful leaders also use their personality when managing, keeping their sense of humor and admitting mistakes. Perhaps most importantly, insightful management can vest individuals with the feeling that the organization's success is their own. This can be accomplished by giving people high levels of responsibility so that they feel their work is an integral factor in the group's achievements.

Another old adage, "lead by example," also rings true. Evidence of this can be seen time and again in the Heroic Age, when grueling work was required, and no doubt there would have been significant problems if the men believed their leaders were not doing their share of the hard labor. Leaders who show dedication, perseverance and hard work inspire their people to do the same.

Finally, there is the all-important issue of raising and maintaining morale. Well thought out scheduling of work, rest, and recreation activities helps people stay focused and productive. Direct communication with individuals or small groups can be a very effective technique for gauging morale and imparting a positive outlook. Also, information that could be damaging to morale should be disbursed carefully and purposefully, while opportunities to raise spirits should be sought out and taken advantage of.

These concepts, used so effectively at the bottom of the world, are global, and can be used by leaders in any type of organization and at any level. Your challenge, as a leader, is to apply the model effectively in your organization so that the men and women who are a part of it reach unprecedented heights of job satisfaction and productivity.

Epilogue

What Happened to the Heroes Of Antarctic Exploration?

Not long before he passed away in 1985, Dick Richards, who had survived the sledging journeys with Joyce and the disappearance of the *Aurora*, recorded a radio interview about his experiences as a member of the Ross Sea Party. Richards detailed the suffering he and the other men endured, including two thousand miles of tortuous depot laying, painful snow blindness, and the terrible effects of scurvy. Interestingly, Richards also noted that his time in Antarctica was the most rewarding period of his life. He had to work hard every day just to keep himself and his crewmates alive—and he found a pure satisfaction in that.

Richards was not alone. For many of the Heroic Age explorers, Antarctica was the site of their greatest achievements, and their connection to the Southern Continent was an indelible part of their lives. Although there is insufficient space here to detail the lives of all the explorers, there are numerous biographies of many of them, including the somewhat lesser known. Below is a therefore abbreviated list of some of the more important figures of the Antarctic, and of the ships they used to get there.

The People

Tom Crean

In September, 1917, Crean married Eileen "Nell" Herlihy, 36, a childhood friend. In April, 1919, Crean was badly injured in an accidental fall aboard the Navy cruiser *Fox*. He suffered a gash to the head that distorted his vision and left him badly bruised. By March 1920 Crean had still not recovered and retired after a twenty-six year career at sea.

Crean returned to his hometown of Annascaul, in County Kerry, Ireland, and settled down to life on land for the first time in decades. A daughter, Mary, had been born in late 1918, followed by Kate in 1920. When Shackleton recruited Crean to serve aboard the Quest, Crean politely declined. A third daughter, Eileen, was born in 1922, but tragically Kate died in 1924.

Tom and Nell opened a bar in Annascaul named the "South Pole Inn." Crean enjoyed talking to locals and visitors, while Nell controlled the day to day operations. Crean soon became known for the same wit and humility he had demonstrated in the Antarctic. In 1938 Crean suffered an appendicitis, but by the time he reached the closest surgeon, at a hospital in Cork more than seventy-five miles distant, he was suffering from a severe infection. He survived for a week, but died on July 27. Tom Crean, 61, was buried next to Kate.

Nell sold The South Pole Inn in 1948, the same year that the film *Scott of the Antarctic* premiered. Nell, Eileen and Mary traveled to Cork to watch the film, in which John Gregson played the role of Tom Crean. Nell Crean died in 1968 at the age of 86. The South Pole Inn closed in 1987, but has since been reopened.

Ernest Joyce

Captain Ernest Joyce spent six months in the hospital and had to wear dark glasses for eighteen months recovering from the snow blindness he suffered as a member of *Aurora's*

Ross Sea Party. Joyce had served with Scott during the *Discovery* Expedition, with Shackleton on the *Nimrod*, and had led the *Aurora's* sledging team after Mackintosh fell ill. Joyce and Dick Richards were the only survivors of the depot laying journeys that took 200 days, a record for sledging travel. During that time they covered 1,900 miles. Joyce died in London in 1940 at the age of sixty-five.

Sir Douglas Mawson

Mawson returned to Antarctica in 1929 as the leader of BANZARE (the British, Australian, and New Zealand Antarctic Research Expedition). Mawson organized the expedition, which received financial support from the three nations as well as private donors. The expedition used Scott's ship, *Discovery*, and airplanes to survey large areas of Antarctica that would be claimed as the Australian Antarctic Territory. BANZARE also focused on scientific research and produced significant amounts of data, especially in the area of marine biology. Mawson's work as an explorer and scientist made him a national hero in Australia, and he is pictured on the country's $100 note. Mawson had a wide variety of interests, including conservation, and he worked hard to have Macquarie Island, located about halfway between Australia and Antarctica, established as a nature sanctuary. He died in 1958 at the age of 76.

Fridtjof Nansen

Nansen resigned his position as Norway's Ambassador to Britain in 1907, hoping to spend more time with his wife Eva and their children, but Eva's death late in the year dramatically changed Nansen's life. The large house they had built at Lysaker as a dream home now became a place of isolation, as Nansen sent the children to stay with friends for long periods of time and threw himself into research and a study of international issues.

He lobbied the Norwegian government to increase defense spending in the years prior to World War I, arguing that a capable defense force would be needed to repel invaders. In

1917-1918, Nansen led a delegation in Washington D.C. that arranged for a loosening of the Allied blockade to permit vital shipments of food to Norway. In 1919, Nansen married Sigrun Munthe, who had recently divorced the artist Gerhard Munthe.

Following the war, the International Red Cross was overwhelmed with the task of repatriating of hundreds of thousands of prisoners of war scattered across Europe and Asia. The newly formed League of Nations undertook the task, and in April 1920, asked Nansen to lead the project. Although he wanted to focus on his scientific studies, Nansen accepted, partly due to his compassion for the prisoners, many of whom were living in deplorable conditions, and also to help establish the League of Nations as an organization that could be effective on an international scale. Nansen was able to generate cooperation between nations that had recently been mortal enemies, even though the situation was further complicated by the distrust of western nations of the new communist government in the Soviet Union. In less than two years, Nansen was able to coordinate the return of 450,000 prisoners of war, many of whom would certainly have died if not for his intervention. Nansen worked closely with various humanitarian organizations and was therefore able to minimize the cost of the prisoner transfers, which pleased the governments involved. Nansen was not paid for his work as High Commissioner of Prisoners of War.

In early 1921, while Nansen was still involved with the prisoners of war, the International Red Cross and the League of Nations asked him to help find homes for the millions of refugees displaced by the war. One of the biggest issues for the refugees was that many did not have official identification. Nansen solved this issue with a new invention, the Nansen Passport, which allowed individuals to cross into any of the multiple nations that accepted it. Nansen also worked tirelessly to alleviate the serious problem of Russian refuges in Turkey, and eventually convinced forty-four countries to accept Turkish refugees.

By 1921 the widespread famine in the Soviet Union, long denied by the government, was finally admitted to the world. International relief efforts began, and Nansen was again called upon to lead. Nansen spoke at the League of Nations, stating "In the name of humanity, in the name of all that is pure and holy, I appeal to you, who yourselves have wives and children at home - think what it means to see women and children die of starvation. From this place I appeal to the governments, to the people of Europe, to the whole world, for help. Hurry - before it is too late to regret." Despite Nansen's inspired pleas, western European governments were unwilling to supply aid to the communists, despite the grave consequences. Disappointed but undeterred, Nansen continued his efforts with his usual intensity. He was eventually able to arrange for the allocation of enough food to save an astonishing amount of Russians from starvation. Estimates have put the number between seven and twenty-two *million*.

After a flood of over one million refugees into Greece from Asia Minor during the Greco-Turkish War (1921-1922), the Greek government sought Nansen's help. He was able to obtain short-term assistance, but also offered a long-term solution: a wide scale population exchange between the two countries. Half a million Turks living in Greece were exchanged for approximately 1.25 million Greeks living in Turkey, thus effectively removing the minority populations of both countries. In December, 1922, Nansen received the Nobel Peace Prize.

In 1925 the League of Nations requested Nansen's assistance in saving what was left of the Armenian population after the genocide of 1915-1923. Nansen envisioned a home for the Armenians at Erivan, and designed political and economic blueprints, predating by two decades work done by the United Nations Technical Assistance Board and the International Bank of Development and Reconstruction. Nansen spent many years in an unrelenting appeal to the citizens and governments of the world for support of the Armenians.

The burden of his humanitarian work during the 1920s took a toll on Nansen. Not only was he unable to devote time to his first love, scientific research, but he was deeply frustrated by the lack of support he received from world leaders in his attempts to help people in need. Nansen's health deteriorated, and he Nansen died of a heart attack at his home in 1930.

Dick Richards

After serving with the Ross Sea Party, Richards returned to his position as Lecturer of Physics and Mathematics at the Ballarat School of Mines and Industries. During World War II he served as an advisor in the production of optical equipment. In 1946 he became Principal of Ballarat and retired in 1958. A year later Ballarat began honoring their top science graduate with the Richard W. Richards medal. In 1984 Richards received praise from Australian Prime Minister Bob Hawke for his tireless efforts in the Antarctic. Dick Richards died in 1985 at the age of ninety-one.

Kathleen Scott

Kathleen Scott remarried in 1922 to Edward Hilton Young, Member of Parliament, and they had one child. Her statues of Robert Scott stand in London and New Zealand, while her statue of Edward Wilson resides in Cheltenham. Her bust of Scott, and other sculptures, can be found at the Scott Polar Research Institute in Cambridge. Kathleen died in 1947.

Sir Peter Scott

In his final letter to Kathleen, Robert Scott asked her to raise their young son Peter with an interest in "natural history." Indeed, Peter became a pioneering member of the conservationist movement, founding and serving as the first chairman of the World Wildlife Fund in 1961, and later founding the Wildfowl and Wetlands Trust. Like his mother, Peter was an accomplished artist, specializing in paintings of birds. He won a bronze medal in sailing at the 1936 Olympic Games in Berlin, and later became a champion glider. He received the Distinguished Service Cross for his actions during World War II, and later became a well-liked television personality on the BBC wildlife show *Look*. In 1973 he became the first conservationist to be knighted. Peter died in 1989 at the age of 79.

Frank Wild

Shackleton's right-hand man settled in South Africa, and worked in various jobs until his death in 1939. The body was cremated and the ashes were to be brought to South Georgia Island to be interred next to Shackleton. With the outbreak of World War II, however, the plans to move Wild's remains were cancelled, and the ashes were lost—until 2011, when Wild's biographer Angie Butler tracked them down in a cemetery in Johannesburg. On November 27, 2011, Wild's ashes were buried next to Shackleton's grave on South Georgia Island. Alexandra Shackleton, Ernest's granddaughter, attended the service, as did Frank Wild's great nieces and nephews.

Sir James Wordie

After being wounded near Armentieres during the Battle of Lys in 1918, just weeks before the armistice, Wordie was appointed to the position of Lecturer in Cambridge University's Geology Department, beginning a distinguished career in academia. He also continued the adventurous life of an explorer and mountaineer. In the 1920s and 1930s he led expeditions to Greenland and the Canadian Arctic, married and raised a family of five, and continued to teach. In 1937 Wordie was appointed Chairman of the Scott Polar Research Institute.

During World War II he served with Naval Intelligence, and in 1946 returned to the Antarctic, including a visit to Elephant Island in 1947. In 1950 he was elected President of St. John's College, Cambridge, and Master of the College in 1952. Wordie also served as vice-chairman of the Everest Committee and chairman of the British Mountaineering Council. In 1957 Wordie was knighted for his role as a polar explorer and research. He retired in 1959 at died in 1962 at the age of 72.

Frank Worsley

Following World War I, Worsley returned to the polar regions in 1926 as part of the British Arctic Expedition, exploring the region between Franz Joseph Land and Spitsbergen Island. During World War II he served in a variety of roles, including working with the Red Cross in both France and Norway. Worsley died in 1943.

The Ships

Discovery

Discovery's adventures did not end with its return from the Antarctic in 1904. It traveled the world as a cargo ship for the Hudson Bay Company, and was used to transport munitions to Russia during World War I. *Discovery* headed south again in 1925 to research the population and migratory habits of whales as a prelude to conservationism and regulation of commercial whaling. *Discovery* also participated in BANZARE (1929-1931) the British, Australian, New Zealand Antarctic Research Expedition, led by Douglas Mawson.

For almost fifty years, *Discovery* served as a training ship for Sea Scouts and the Royal Navy Reserve, but she was in bad shape by the late 1970s. A grant of half a million pounds by the Maritime Trust helped restore the ship, which was returned to its birthplace of Dundee, Scotland in 1986. Since 1993 *Discovery* has been berthed at Discovery Point in Dundee where it is open to visitors.

Fram, Gjoa and *Maud*

After reaching the South Pole, Amundsen planned to return to the Arctic with the *Fram*, but the outbreak of World War I in 1914 stopped the expedition. By 1925 the ship was in poor condition, but Otto Sverdup championed the ship's cause, and attempted to raise money as the first chairman of the *Fram* Committee. Sverdup lived to see restorations begin in 1930, but he died in November of that year. In 1935 a museum was built specifically to house the *Fram* indoors. Fram House opened in Oslo on May 20, 1936. The King and Crown Prince attended, as did Oscar Wisting, who had reached both Poles with

Amundsen. Today the Fram Museum is a major tourist attraction in Oslo. The *Gjoa*, the ship Amundsen used to traverse the Northwest Passage, is also on display at the museum.

Another of Amundsen's ships, the *Maud*, sunk in the shallow waters of Cambridge Bay, Nunavut in 1930, and the partially exposed hulk had been deteriorating for over eighty years. In 2012, the Maud Returns Home project, led by Norwegian artist and historian Jan Wanggaard, received permission from the Canadian Cultural Property Export Review Board to salvage the ship and return it to Norway. In July, 2015, efforts began to salvage the *Maud* with the plan of returning it to Norway in 2016, exactly one hundred years after its launch.

Nimrod

The *Nimrod* became a coal supply ship and was lost in the North Sea in January 1919 during a fierce storm. After becoming stuck on the Barber Sands off Norfolk, the ship was battered until it was crushed and sank, along with ten members of the crew.

Terra Nova

After her return from Antarctica, the *Terra Nova* was used as a sealer and supply ship primarily in Newfoundland and Canada. In September, 1942 it was transporting supplies to American military bases on Greenland when in struck ice that caused significant damage. The U.S. Coast Guard cutter *Southwind* rescued the crew of twenty-four, but the ship was lost. A few objects from the *Terra Nova* had been removed in 1913 upon its return to Cardiff and can still be seen today. The figurehead is housed at the National Museum of Wales, and the binnacle, a navigational instrument, is on display at the Pierhead Building at the Port of Cardiff, close to the *Terra Nova's* departure point of 1910. The ship's bell was kept by Dr. Atkinson, and was given to the Scott Polar Research Institute (SPRI) at the University of Cambridge in 1952.

In November, 1995, SPRI held a celebration to honor the 75th Anniversary of its founding. Included among the almost four hundred guests was Lady Philippa Scott, widow of Robert and Kathleen's son Peter, and Phillipa and Peter's children Falcon Scott and Dr. Dafila Scott. Shackleton's granddaughter Alexandra Bergel was also in attendance, as were descendants of Dr. Edward Wilson and Frank Debenham. The *Terra Nova's* bell was rung at the event.

In July, 2012, researchers from the Schmidt Ocean Institute were performing tests of their seabed mapping equipment from their flagship, the R/V *Falkor*, off the southern coast of Greenland. The site was chosen for its shallow depth and because the ocean floor was expected to reveal a variety of features that would effectively test the Institute's echosounding gear. Technicians were aware that the *Terra Nova* had gone down in the area, and used the believed location of the wreck as a focal point for the test area. An object was detected about 1,000 meters beneath the surface, with an approximate length of 57 meters, the same as the *Terra Nova*. A submersible camera recorded images of a wrecked wooden vessel, and researchers were able to identify the *Terra Nova* by matching the new pictures with historical photos.

The governments of the United Kingdom, Denmark and the United States, working with the Schmidt Ocean Institute, agreed that the discovery of the *Terra Nova* would be announced publicly, but the exact location of the ship would not be revealed to safeguard the wreckage. After the find was disclosed, some news reports suggested that the vessel had been found purely by accident, which was not the case. Scott and Wilson would have been proud to know that the *Terra Nova* was found by researchers dedicated to scientific discovery.

BIBLIOGRAPHY

Amundsen, Roald. *The South Pole: An Account of the Norwegian Expedition in the* Fram, *1910–12* (Volumes I and II). London: John Murray, 1912.

Bickel, Lennard. *Shackleton's Forgotten Men: The Untold Tragedy of the Endurance Epic.* New York: Thunder's Mouth Press, 2000.

Bernacchi, Louis. *Saga of the Discovery.* London: Blackie and Son, 1938.

Cox, Lynne. *South with the Sun.* New York: Alfred A. Knopf, 2011.

Cherry-Garrard, Apsley. *The Worst Journey in the World.* London: Constable, 1922.

Mill, Robert. *The Life of Sir Ernest Shackleton.* Boston: Little, Brown and Company, 1923.

Morrell, Margot, and Capparell, Stephanie. *Shackleton's Way: Leadership Lessons from the Great Antarctic Explorer.* New York: Viking, 2001.

Perkins, Dennis N.T. *Leading at the Edge: Leadership Lesson from the Extraordinary Saga of Shackleton's Antarctic Expedition.* New York: AMACOM, 2000.

Scott, Robert. *Scott's Last Expedition*. London: Smith, Elder and Co., 1913.

Scott, Robert. *The Voyage of the "Discovery"*. London: Smith, Elder and Co., 1905.

Shackleton, Ernest. *South: The Story of Shackleton's Last Expedition 1914-1917*. New York: MacMillan, 1920.

Shackleton, Ernest. *The Heart of the Antarctic: Being the Story of the British Antarctic Expedition, 1907-1909*. London: Ballantyne and Co., 1909.

Wild, Frank. *Shackleton's Last Voyage. The Story of the Quest*. London: Cassell and Company, 1923.

Wilson, Edward. *Diary of the "Discovery" Expedition*. London: Blandford Press, 1966.

Wilson, Edward. *South Pole Odyssey: Selections from the Antarctic Diaries of Edward Wilson*. Poole, England: Blandford Press, 1982.

Wilson, Edward. *Diary of the 'Terra Nova' Expedition to the Antarctic, 1910-1912*. London: Blandford, 1972.

Smith, Michael. *Polar Crusader: A Life of Sir James Wordie*. Edinburgh: Birlinn Limited, 2004.

Worsley, Frank. *Shackleton's Boat Journey*. New York: W.W. Norton and Company, 1933.

Worsley, Frank. *Endurance: An Epic of Polar Adventure*. New York: W.W. Norton and Company, 1931.

www.ingramcontent.com/pod-product-compliance
Lightning Source LLC
Chambersburg PA
CBHW051649170526
45167CB00001B/395